GW00733050

▶ FOCUS ON ◀

P·E·T

Preliminary English Test

TEACHER'S BOOK

DIANA L FRIED-BOOTH

Longman

Pearson Education Limited
Edinburgh Gate Harlow
Essex CM20 2JE
and Associated Companies throughout the world.

www.longman-elt.com

First edition © HarperCollins Publishers Limited 1991
This edition © Addison Wesley Longman Limited 1996
Fifth impression 2000

All rights reserved; no part of this publication
may be reproduced, stored in any retrieval system,
or transmitted in any form or by any means, electronic,
mechanical, photocopying, recording or otherwise,
without the prior written permission of the publishers.

Set in 10/11pt Sabon

Printed in Malaysia, PJB

ISBN 0 17 557120 1

Contents

The colour prompts for the oral component of the
Practice Test are in the middle of this Teacher's Book.

Map of Focus on PET Student's Book				
UNIT	TOPICS	LEAD-IN	READING SKILLS	WRITING SKILLS
1	People Places Directions Friendships Relationships	Nationalities *p.6*	*'A Child of the Forest' p.8* Dictionary definitions *p.8* Signs *p.11*	Message *p.12*
2	Homes Houses Family life Accommodation	Different kinds of homes *p.14*	Labelling drawings *p.14* Advertisements *p.15* Notices *p.16* *Debbie's letter p.16*	Informal letter *p.21*
3	Shops Shopping Services	Currencies and exchange rates *p.24*	*Markets p.26* Advertisements *p.28*	Short report *p.25* Message *p.29* Ordering by post *p.30* Town plan *p.30*
4	Food Drink Restaurants	Picture puzzle *p.32* Guessing game *p.32*	Menu *p.33* Letter *p.35* Restaurant advertisements *p.38*	Menus *p.35* Questionnaire *p.39* Short report *p.39* Recipes *p.39* Letter *p.40*
5	Health Lifestyles	Jokes *p.42* Labelling parts of the body *p.42*	*Health p.43* *'Lifestyles' p.46* *'Reactivart' p.49*	Notes during an interview *p.46* Daily routine *p.46* Letter *p.49*
6	Holidays Travel Hotels Weather	Countries and capitals *p.52*	Accommodation advertisements *p.53* Postcards *p.54* *'Inter-Rail' p.59*	Booking accommodation *p.54* Postcards *p.55* Fact sheet *p.60*
7	Education Politics Language learning	Matching people and occupations *p.62*	*'Travellers' p.63* Signs and notices *p.68*	Report based on diagrams *p.66* Questions *p.68* Letter *p.68* Expanding headlines *p.69*
8	Entertainment Media Famous people	Visual puzzle *p.72* Photographs of famous people *p.72*	*'Capital Radio' p.73* Advertisements *p.74* Programme schedules *p.80* *'Street Scene' p.81* Headlines *p.82*	Table *p.76* Questions *p.80* Booking form *p.84*
9	Work Sports Hobbies Animals and pets	Cartoon *p.86* Matching people and hobbies *p.86*	*'Robin Knox-Johnson' p.88* *'Dame Judi Dench' p.89* *'James Warren' p.90* Instructions *p.95*	CV *p.91* Letter *p.96*

Map of Focus on PET Student's Book

LISTENING SKILLS	SPEAKING SKILLS	GRAMMAR	VOCABULARY	FURTHER PRACTICE and PET related Question

Class register *p.7*
 Directions *p.11*
	Pairwork role-play
	 - interview *p.7*
	 - directions *p.11*
		Reported speech *p.10*	Family relationships *p.13*	Writing (Part 2):
				   Form filling *p.116*
				 Reported speech *p.117*
				 Writing (Part 3):
				   Informal letter *p.117*

Information sheet *p.18*
 Matching visual
   information *p.22*
	Accommodation *p.17*
	 Preferences *p.17*
	 Planning a room *p.20*
	 Photograph *p.21*
		Uncountable nouns
		   p.19
		 there + be p.19
			Buildings *p.23*
			 Signs *p.23*
				Reading (Part 1):
				   Notices *p.118*
				 Writing (Part 3):
				   Informal letter *p.119*

Services and prices
   p.26
 Table *p.30*
	Shopping habits *p.25*
	 Recommending shops
	   p.30
		Instructions - zero
		   conditionals *p.27*
		 *To have something
		   done p.28*
		 Need + infinitive *p.28*
		 Need + gerund *p.28*
			Shops *p.31*
			 Services *p.31*
				Reading (Part 5):
				   Gapped text *p.120*
				 Oral (Part 2):
				   Role-play *p.121*

Food bills *p.33*
 Places to eat *p.36*
	Favourite food and
	   drink *p.35*
	 Using a questionnaire
	   p.39
		Adverbial order *p.36*	Restaurant bill *p.41*	Listening (Part 1):
				   Mini-dialogues *p.122*
				 Writing (Part 3):
				   Competition entry
				   p.123

Doctor's message
   p.45
 'Lifestyles' p.45
 Medical situations
   p.47
	Minor ailments *p.44*
	 Interviewing *p.46*
	 Role-play *p.47*
		Verb base + *-ing p.48*
		 -ing after certain verbs
		   and prepositions
		   p.48
			Major world religions
			   p.50
			 Personal health/
			   hygiene *p.51*
				Reading (Part 1):
				   Notices *p.124*
				 Reading (Part 3):
				   Leaflet *p.125*

Map route *p.52*
 Notes *p.58*
	Planning a holiday
	   p.56
		Passives *p.57*
		 Relative pronouns *p.58*
			Months of the year
			   p.61
			 Seasons *p.61*
				Writing (Part 3):
				   Letter *p.126*
				 Reading (Part 5):
				   Gapped text *p.127*

Notes from a telephone
   conversation *p.67*
 Asking for help *p.70*
	Likes and dislikes -
	   school subjects *p.66*
	 Photograph *p.70*
		Prepositions *p.64*
		 Modals - *must/mustn't/
		   ought to/should/
		   have to/don't have to
		   p.65*
			Related vocabulary
			   p.71
			 Dictionary definitions
			   p.71
				Reading (Part 4):
				   Extract *p.128*
				 Oral (Part 3):
				   Describing a photo
				   p.129

Plans *p.78*
 Booking form *p.83*
	Favourite programmes
	   etc. *p.73*
	 Role play *p.80*
	 Reasons for choices
	   p.80
	 Making decisions *p.84*
		Phrasal verbs *p.78*
		 Imperatives *p.79*
			Theatres *p.85*
			 Tickets *p.85*
			 Entertainment *p.85*
				Listening (Part 2):
				   Factual information
				   p.130
				 Writing (Part 3):
				   Video choice *p.131*

Hobbies *p.87*
 Sports report *p.92*
	Jobs *p.90; p.91*
	 Balloon debate *p.93*
	 Persuading people
	   p.96
		Present perfect tense
		   with certain adverbs
		   and prepositions
		   p.93
			Symbols *p.97*
			 Punctuation marks
			   p.97
			 Abbreviations *p.97*
				Listening (Part 4):
				   Dialogue *p.132*
				 Writing (Part 1):
				   Transformations *p.132*

PET at a Glance

Reading Paper

	PART 1	PART 2	PART 3	PART 4	PART 5
TASK	5 multiple-choice questions based on signs, adverts, notices etc.	5 multiple-match questions based on 8 short texts	10 true/false questions based on one text	5 multiple-choice questions based on a short text	gapped text with 10 multiple-choice questions
SKILL	identifying the main message	detailed comprehension	picking out the main points from what may be redundant	understanding a writer's intention, opinion and attitude	understanding structure, grammar and vocabulary

Writing Paper

	PART 1	PART 2	PART 3
TASK	rewriting 5 short sentences	filling in a form (10 questions)	writing an informal letter based on a written and/or visual prompt
SKILL	understanding simple grammatical structures	ability to supply basic personal information and short responses in the form of a number or a few words	ability to express suggestions, needs, hopes, wishes, regrets, short descriptions, plans etc.

Listening Paper

	PART 1	PART 2	PART 3	PART 4
TASK	7 visual multiple-choice questions for each short monologue/dialogue, including a written prompt	6 multiple-choice questions usually based on an informational monologue	gapped text with 6 questions usually based on a monologue which contains some redundant material	6 true/false questions based on a dialogue
SKILL	identifying a specific or significant point	understanding detail and picking out specific information	understanding the main points from what may be incidental	understanding the opinion and attitudes expressed by the speakers

Speaking Test (taken by candidates in pairs)

	PART 1	PART 2	PART 3	PART 4
TASK	introducing, greeting, finding out about one's partner	taking part in a simulated situation based on simple visual material	describing and briefly comparing two photos	expressing and discussing individual reactions to the topics raised by the photos
SKILL	exchanging basic personal information	ability to make plans, choices, discuss arrangements, reach decisions etc.	responding to visual material on any topic within the PET syllabus	expressing opinions and attitudes based on personal experience

Introduction

Focus on PET provides a complete, integrated course covering all the component skills required to pass the *Cambridge Preliminary English Test*. *Focus on PET* has been thoroughly revised and updated to bring it into line with the changes to the layout of the papers, the question types and the Speaking Test which can now only be taken by pairs of candidates.

The PET was introduced in 1980, substantially revised in 1987 and has now been further revised in the light of the new Threshold Level 1990 document. The changes to the format of the papers as well as to the order of some of the questions within the Reading Paper take effect from March 1996 onwards. The PET tests all four skills – speaking, listening, reading, and writing – within a communicative framework. It assumes prior study of up to approximately 350 hours of English so that students will have reached a language level best described as 'early intermediate'. This course book builds on a basic knowledge of grammar, structure and vocabulary which will have been attained in the first year or two of a general English language course, and directs students towards the tasks expected in the PET itself.

The PET syllabus is closely linked to that of the Council of Europe's Threshold Level in terms of functions, notions and communicative tasks; grammar and structure; topics and vocabulary.

The emphasis of the language tested in the PET is on 'real life' usage, so that candidates can always expect the tasks to reflect a meaningful context and, where appropriate, meaningful interaction. Some of the authentic reading source material will not be heavily modified in any way, as this would destroy the essence of the material. Students will encounter a similar range of authentic material in *Focus on PET*. The unit-by-unit teaching notes make a clear distinction between the language required at PET level for productive purposes (i.e. which students are expected to use) and the language required for receptive purposes (which students are expected to recognise but not produce). Over and above this, in authentic materials there are always likely to be certain vocabulary items which fall outside the PET level, but which need to be kept if sources are to retain their original character. Whether or not a student takes the PET, the largely authentic material in *Focus on PET* will provide a stimulating and enjoyable course at an early intermediate level because they mirror experience of English in everyday life.

The materials aim to appeal to teenagers and young adults, but the teacher's notes allow for adaptation wherever appropriate, as PET is actually taken by a very wide age-range. This course focuses on British English, but it should also be noted that American lexis is perfectly acceptable in the PET. Teachers should encourage their students to use whichever is more familiar, but students must be consistent in their usage.

◆ What is the structure of PET?

The PET consists of four sections: reading, writing, listening and speaking. The reading and writing paper takes 1½ hours, and the listening paper approximately 30 minutes with an additional 12 minutes to allow candidates to transfer their answers from the question paper to the answer sheet.

The different skills are tested in a variety of ways. On the Reading Paper, Parts 1–5 focus on a range of reading skills. Parts 1–3 on the Writing Paper are similarly designed to test a range of productive skills and the Listening Paper, which has four Parts, covers a range of listening skills. The Speaking Test which is taken separately – not necessarily on the same day, but to fit in with each centre's arrangements – is described in the notes for the Practice Test on page 44.

On page 7 there is an overview of the structure of the PET to enable teachers to see at a glance the component parts of each Section.

Teachers wanting further information about the Test and details of the six fixed dates throughout the year when the PET can be taken should write to:

The Director
English as a Foreign Language
Syndicate Buildings
1 Hills Road
Cambridge CB1 2EU
UK

Each section of the test is equally weighted and contributes 25% of the total mark. As each PET test will vary very slightly in its detail there can be no blanket marking scheme. Teachers interested in how one PET may be marked can refer to the Practice Test marking scheme on pages 40–44. There is no minimum pass mark for each section, but a cumulative pass mark for the complete test will probably be approximately 70%. UCLES awards two pass grades (*pass with merit and pass*) and two fail grades (*narrow fail and ungraded*). It is not conducive to effective teaching and test preparation to worry unduly about rigid numerical marks and how they will translate into PET pass marks. A candidate who is able to cope reasonably well with all the tasks throughout the test should find that she/he will be successful.

◆ How to use the course

The course consists of 10 units and a bank of further practice material. The first nine units focus on the range of topics required by the PET syllabus, so that each unit concentrates on theme-related material. The Student's Book has simplified headings in some cases, which are more fully expanded in the Teacher's Book. For example, Unit 7 in the Student's Book is entitled *Education*, whereas in the Teacher's Book it is explained that this unit also covers the vocabulary and related functions for language learning and politics.

The units are loosely graded so that they become increasingly more complex and more closely matched to the actual PET task types towards the end of the course. Unit 10 is a final practice test. This Teacher's Book includes a detailed marking scheme and student sample answers where appropriate.

Each of the nine teaching units encompasses a range of skills, but the emphasis on each skill varies from unit to unit so that, for example, one unit may give more practice in reading and another in listening. Reference to the Map (on pages 4–5) which details the components of each unit shows this distribution of skills. The various sections of each unit are best presented sequentially, as many of the tasks are interrelated (although the Vocabulary section may be exploited as flexibly as teachers wish – see below and separate unit notes).

The *Lead-in* sections are designed to stimulate an awareness of the main topic in a variety of ways and will encourage students to identify with the subject matter. It is important that teachers prepare the introduction to each unit as carefully as possible so that students' imagination is fired from the beginning. Again the detailed notes on each unit suggest ways in which material can be extended if there is sufficient teaching time available.

There is a wide range of *reading* texts from a variety of sources. Some of the texts in the early part of the course are relatively simple. In the later units teachers should look carefully at the unit notes for guidance in training their students to guess at what is unknown and to disregard redundant or irrelevant information. These skills are vital in coping with the actual PET, and the course is designed so that students gain additional practice in these skills in the Further Practice sections (see below).

The *writing* material is geared to the kind of tasks that students can expect to encounter in the PET, and for this reason the majority of tasks are either devised within a clear framework or are based on stimulus material. It should be apparent that students' imagination, whilst always an asset in writing tasks, is not of crucial importance, and they should therefore feel able to tackle the tasks by relying on their own daily experience.

The *listening* material is recorded on two cassettes, and is reproduced in tapescripts which can be found on pages 49–63 of this Teacher's Book. It is taken from both authentic and scripted sources. Depending on the students' 'entry level' to the course and on their 'listening confidence', teachers may prefer to present the listening materials in more manageable portions during the early part of the course. For example, half the class can be asked to listen for one set of information and the other half for a different set (see unit notes for further suggestions.) Teachers should feel able to play or pause the tape as often as is necessary at the beginning of the course, but should bear in mind that by the time they have reached Unit 5 they should have weaned their students away from relying on hearing the taped material more than twice. (For information on how to use the cassettes, see the notes at the beginning of the Tapescripts on page 49.)

As students must take the Speaking section of the test in pairs, the ability to work together is emphasised from the very beginning of the course. Wherever possible students should be encouraged to work together, listening to each other and learning to interact naturally. The instruction to *work with a partner* should always be followed so that students develop their pairwork skills throughout the course and ideally work with different partners on each task.

The skills needed for the *speaking* section of the PET, although deliberately highlighted in some parts of the course, underlie the communicative nature of the entire course, and suggestions are made throughout the teaching notes for potential follow-up with a range of speaking activities.

The *grammar* sections of the course focus on a wide range of key language items which students are expected to know for the PET. As this is not a course for beginners the list of items covered is not comprehensive, so teachers may feel the need to provide supplementary practice from their regular reference sources if students have specific weaknesses (e.g. the use of definite/indefinite articles).

At the end of each unit there is a section which is entitled *Know your Vocabulary*. This focuses on lexical items related to the topic of the unit. It is not necessary to wait until the end of the unit before tackling this material. The teacher's notes make it clear that in some cases it may be desirable to focus on all or some of the material at an earlier stage in the unit, as one way of highlighting certain points.

At various points throughout a unit there are references to *Further Practice* sections which are compiled at the back of the Student's Book. These sections give specific test practice, and teachers are free to decide when to incorporate these into their teaching plan. In some cases it may be desirable to delay using the Further Practice section until later in the course. There is no one way to exploit these sections, but their purpose is to reinforce the work covered in each unit and to focus more directly on the PET question types.

The student sample answers which are included on pages 40–48 are intended to give some guidance on acceptable standards and should not be regarded as definitive models in any way. Teachers should try and assess their individual student's work in the light of what they as teachers know about the PET, and judge each student's work on its own merits in the light of these criteria.

It is hoped that teachers and students using this course will find the materials lively and stimulating, and that preparing for the PET will prove an enjoyable, useful, and entertaining way of learning English.

Unit 1 People and Places

This unit covers the basic skills required in all sections of the PET: to identify oneself and others – to spell, for example, one's name and/or address; to identify family relationships; to give and respond to directions.

◆ Lead-in (p. 6)

1 If you are meeting the class for the first time you can use some of these questions before allowing students to open their books. Identify yourself and your nationality (if appropriate).

Try to make sure that students learn to stress polysyllabic words correctly. The vocabulary section at the end of each unit will help to reinforce this aspect of oral practice, but it is a good idea to emphasise the importance of rhythm, stress and intonation in terms of making oneself understood as early as possible. Additional notes are included in this first unit throughout most of the sub-sections in order to help less experienced teachers. More experienced teachers will have their own 'pet' techniques!

1, 2 The cards from the card game 'Happy Families' and the photographs of different nationalities are designed to broaden the practice and to highlight the differences between the noun, e.g. *Algeria*, and the adjective, *Algerian*.

Give students the basic rules, e.g.

America	American	Italy	Italian
Jamaica	Jamaican	Poland	Polish
Brazil	Brazilian	Spain	Spanish
India	Indian		

remembering to point out that there are always exceptions, e.g. *France – French, Greece – Greek*! If exercise 2 proves difficult, try giving the initial letter of each nationality to speed up the task.

Key: (left to right, top to bottom) Spanish, Japanese, Malaysian, Swiss, French, Italian

◆ Listening (p. 7)

Note: Longer recordings, like the one here, are given only once on the tape. You will need to rewind the tape to allow students to listen again.

3 Before you play the tape make sure the students understand the headings on the class register. You may also need to revise question forms once again if you feel the Lead-in has indicated that the students are not as familiar with the structures as they need to be.

Tell your students that *surname* and *family name* are interchangeable. (*First name* is more common than *Christian name* on application forms.)

DoB is a common abbreviation for 'Date of Birth'. Make sure your students recognise the convention of putting *day + month + year*.

At the beginning of the tape students will hear the teacher refer to herself as *tutor*. This word is often used when someone teaches small groups of students, but is not a word which students need to learn at this level.

Encourage the class just to listen the first time you play the tape, without necessarily writing anything. If students have difficulty at this early stage of the course in getting down their answers, encourage them to listen for only one or two pieces of information at a time. Or divide the class into small groups with each group listening for specific pieces of information. Try to make sure that students develop confidence in handling small amounts of information before you move on to playing more extended listening tasks.

Key: Gonzalez; Gardens; 88431; Spanish; Antonelli, 11-4-73; 259 Sadler Street; ......; Italian

◆ Speaking and Writing (p. 7)

4 When completing forms and questionnaires the answers do not need to be in complete sentences. An example of a completed form is printed on page 41 as one of the sample answers to the Practice Test (Unit 10).

Remind your students that a signature is **not** printed.

◆ Reading (pp. 8–9)

5, 6 Before starting this reading exercise encourage the students to look at the map and the location of the Forest of Dean. The majority of English counties end with *-shire* e.g. Oxfordshire, Lancashire etc. It is worth pointing this out for receptive purposes only, and perhaps asking students to discuss the equivalent (if any) for county in their own country, e.g. *département* in France.

Ask students to guess (if they don't already know) the location of Bristol, Birmingham and London before labelling them!

Note: All the dictionary extracts in the course are adapted from the *Collins COBUILD Essential English Dictionary*.

7 Key: 1 No **2** Yes **3** Yes **4** No **5** No **6** Yes

8 The inclusion here of a gapped reading text closely related to what the students have just read is designed to give maximum support (at this early stage) in tackling this kind of exercise (Part 5 of the Reading Paper). Students can check their own answers by looking at the key, or you might choose to check it as a class exercise in order to highlight any common difficulties.

Key: **1** lived   **2** in   **3** had   **4** to   **5** which   **6** up
7 but   **8** left   **9** Although   **10** at

Note: Although and *though* can be used in the same way (when they are conjunctions), but *though* is more informal.

◆ Grammar (p. 10)

Note: Explanations in the Grammar sections are marked with pink dots in the margin (see 10, 12, 13 in the Student's Book).

9 *Reported speech*: If your students are not familiar with how to form the past and past perfect tenses then you will need to pre-teach this before moving on to exercise 10. Choose the verbs which occur in this section: *do, have, want, grow, leave, sell, ask* as well as the verb *to be*.

Other questions could include:

Did you live in a large house?
Did you come from a rich family?
Did anyone else live with your family?
Did you want to leave school?
When did you write your first book?
Do you like music?

11 Obviously the age and status of the students will affect your own form of question, i.e. *What do you want to do when . . . ?* or *What did you want to do when . . . ?*

Draw students' attention to the fact that in reported speech *if/whether* are used when there is no question word like *why* or *where*.

13 Once the students have practised these and worked through the exercise, encourage the class to discuss what the grammar rules are for reported speech before they write in their own formula in the box provided.

If you prefer, allow the students to write the formula in their mother tongue, provided it is clear that the rule will be remembered – something relatively simple – such as:

present	→	*past*
past	→	*past perfect*

with one or two of their own examples.

The Further Practice exercise on reported speech (page 117) can be left for revision until a later stage in the course (if appropriate) as a way of refreshing students' memories.

◆ Listening and speaking (p. 11)

14 You may want to refer to maps of the students' own town/city as a way of introducing this topic. For initial oral practice use what is to come on the tape as a guide, in conjunction with landmarks which are familiar to the students. For example, 'Sushila, where is the cinema – is it near the river?' or 'How do I get from the museum to the car park?'

◆ Reading (p. 11)

17 The signs, whilst being loosely topic-related for the purposes of this unit, are primarily designed to introduce the student to Part 1 of the Reading Paper, which requires candidates to understand public signs and notices through a multiple-choice question. A couple of the notices here, however, are minimal: P for Parking is recognised internationally, whereas M for Motorway is not. The questions in the PET will always have a message which relies on a few words as opposed to one single letter – as in the example in exercise 18.

Key: **1** This sign is sometimes placed on the roadside after roadworks have ended
2 a street sign indicating parking is allowed
3 direction to a motorway
4 from a leaflet advertising a bus company

18   Key: to apologise for any inconvenience

◆ Writing (p. 12)

20 Before asking students to write their own messages, ask them to look at the examples. Practice is given in writing messages as one way of giving students confidence to cope with the letter writing task in Part 3 of the Writing Paper.

21 Beaulieu, pronounced (/'bjuːliː/). Before the students write their message, get them to talk about what they imagine Beaulieu has to offer (e.g. old cars to look at and ride in, gardens, picnic areas, lake, cafés and restaurants). The message need not to be more than 30/40 words long.

Further practice in writing messages is given at the bottom of page 117. Ideally this should be set as a homework task.

◆ Know your Vocabulary (p. 13)

22 Each unit ends with a section which is designed to introduce and consolidate vocabulary and other language parts relevant to the theme of the unit, but which may not have been directly focused upon during the unit. Students should always be encouraged to record their own examples where appropriate, so that they can identify with the stimulus material as much as possible.

23 Key: 1A 2F 3E 4C 5D 6B 7H 8G

24 Each of these 'Know your vocabulary' sections also includes an exercise on pronunciation. Students are required to listen to the teacher's pronunciation in order to mark the main word stress(es). One-syllable words are included so that you can draw your student's attention to the fact that diphthongs are not to be perceived as separate sounds. Remind students about the 'silent' final *e* that affects the length of the vowel sound, but sometimes leads learners to make pronunciation mistakes. You may like to encourage your students to put a faint pencil slash through words which prove persistently problematic, e.g. square (/skwɛə/)

Make sure that the students mark up the main word stresses in their own books as they listen, and check that this has been done correctly by getting them to repeat the word for you after a period of time. This kind of follow-up should only take a few minutes and could be fitted in at any time convenient to your teaching programme.

Checklist:

1 married	4 nationality	7 niece	10 square
2 single	5 husband	8 nephew	11 junction
3 relative	6 wife	9 crossing	12 crossroads

Unit 2 Homes

♦ *Lead-in (p. 14)*

1 Use the pictures to stimulate discussion. It is not necessary for students to learn the names of these kinds of homes, apart from *cottage* and *hut* which they are expected to know at this level.

Key: 1 cottage – worldwide (this particular one is in Ireland and has a roof made of straw)
2 mud hut – this example is an African Bantu hut and has designs painted on the walls
3 igloo – built by Eskimos in the Arctic
4 lighthouse – also worldwide, although may be less common as a home
5 house on stilts – in this case in the Philippine islands
6 houseboat – found worldwide

apartment flat

Other possible suggestions for kinds of houses might include tent, cave, caravan or trailer, windmill, junk, but it is not necessary to explore these (or others) if they do not arise spontaneously out of class discussion.

This lead-in provides another opportunity to exploit names of countries and nationality adjectives; it is especially important that students can both say and write their own nationality adjective.

♦ *Reading and Writing (pp. 14–15)*

2 If your students do not already know these words, encourage them to ask each other, or to look them up in a dictionary. Make sure that they learn *lounge*, *kitchen*, and *carpet*.

Words outside the level are included. This is because candidates are likely to encounter these in the PET (though they will not be directly tested). It is important to train your students to make sensible guesses when they come across words they don't know, and not to panic or to be put off by words they don't initially recognise.

utility room   Key: lounge

bungalow   carpet   kitchen/diner   double-glazed   fitted kitchen

Note: Double glazing is not standard in most UK housing.

A utility room usually has an additional sink, plumbing for a washing machine, and extra storage space.

A fitted kitchen is already equipped with cupboards, sink, fridge, stove – often designed so that all the units match.

3 Before beginning this task it might be a good idea to discuss with your class the use of abbreviations in general and, if appropriate, those commonly used in their mother tongue. You may also need to pre-teach *equip/ped*, for recognition purposes only.

The abbreviations used in the advertisements are: *bed* (B, D, F) – bedroom; *c.h.* (D) – central heating; *Tel:* (D, E, F) – telephone; *No.* (A) – number.

4   Key: Susan and Tom – B; Mrs Jackson – E; Ms Blum – G; Mr Miles – D.

5 Before asking students to do this task it may be useful to look at some of the vocabulary from exercises 25 and 26 (p.23) Exercise 5 may then be started in class and written up for homework.

◆ Reading (p. 16)

6, 7, 8 How you tackle this section will depend on the age of your students. You may want to emphasise the teenage point of view or a more adult role. In either case, encourage your class to discuss the kinds of problems that can arise between parents and their children. What sort of things do teenagers usually complain about regarding their parents and living at home? What are/were your students' experiences as teenagers? What about the problems of being parents at this stage of an adolescent's development?

◆ Reading (pp. 16–17)

9 You may want to discuss the role of magazine problem pages as a warm-up activity before asking your class to read this letter.

10 This task is directly related to Part 4 of the Reading Paper in which candidates have to identify the source of a text. In addition to the written clues there may also be visual clues which students need to be alert to. Here, of course, students are told that the text is a letter so no detective work is necessary. But you need to direct students' attention to the informal style of the letter and the tone of protest and complaint. The structure of the letter and the vocabulary are fairly simple and for the most part sound like spoken English.

11   Key: 1 F   2 T   3 T   4 F   5 F   6 T

12 In addition to the pairwork activities you may want to develop a mini role-play involving Debbie, her parents, a friend of the family, Debbie's teacher or one of Debbie's friends. Two or three students could act out the scene of an argument based on the information in the letter and extend it along lines suggested by the rest of the class from the pairwork discussion activities.

◆ Speaking and Writing (p. 17)

13 If your students already know this information about each other, use the opening exchange to practise stress and intonation, and if there is time set up a class survey in which the students (in small groups) find out how many of the class live in flats/houses/in the city centre/in the suburbs.

15 Remind your class that their 'reasons' do not have to be written as complete sentences. This written task can be followed up by getting students to exchange their comments, to see how far they may share or differ in their reasons.

◆ Listening (p. 18)

16 Before you play the tape ask students to look at the questionnaires. Discuss the kind of information they would expect to hear in order to complete the questionnaires. As there are two people being interviewed, you may wish to divide the tape into separate parts, focusing on one questionnaire at a time. In any case there is a natural break in terms of the background office noise.

Make sure your students understand the words *furnished* and *unfurnished*. Pre-teach *rent*. (This is consolidated, and contrasted with *for sale*, in exercise 27, but there is no reason why it cannot be highlighted at this point.)

Note: *Hire* is used for e.g. a boat or a bicycle, where you pay a fixed sum in order to use the item for a period of time. If you *rent* something, e.g. a room or a flat, you usually pay a sum of money at regular intervals.

Key:

HOUSEFINDERS
Agency

NAME ...*STOPES*............MR/MRS/MISS/MS

Tel. No. (daytime) ....*247613*..........

House ☐   Flat/Apartment ☐

Rent ☐   price ....
Buy ☑   price *£75,000*
Number of rooms ...*5*........

Furnished ☐   Unfurnished ☐

Central heating ☑   Shower ☐

Garage/parking space ☐   Laundry room ☐

Position ...*City centre. Near station and bus route.*

HOUSEFINDERS
Agency

NAME ..*JONES*...............MR/MRS/MISS/MS

Tel. No. (daytime) ......✓

House ☐   Flat/Apartment ☑

Rent ☑   price *£120 per week*
Buy ☐   price ....
Number of rooms ...*4*........

Furnished ☑   Unfurnished ☐

Central heating ☐   Shower ☑

Garage/parking space ☑   Laundry room ☐

Position *Outside city centre. Not in country. Not noisy.*

◆ Grammar (p. 19)

17 As an introduction to this section you may wish to ask your class whether these words are countable or uncountable in their **mother tongue**. This may help to clarify the focus of the exercise and the fact that none of these words have plural forms.

18 Key: 1 news   2 furniture   3 countryside... scenery   4 money   5 traffic   6 accommodation   7 transport   8 information

19 This exercise is designed to remind students of the way in which we can express whether or not something **exists** by using *there is/are* before the subject. Knowledge of this grammatical pattern is often tested in Part 1 of the Writing Paper.

Key: 1 are   2 There are   3 is   4 There is   5 There are

◆ Speaking and Writing (pp. 20 and 21)

20, 21, 22 These exercises are designed to recycle some of the key vocabulary introduced in this unit, and at the same time to incorporate some of the skills required in the speaking and writing parts of the PET.

21 This exercise enables students to work in pairs, choosing and planning how they would furnish a room. You should encourage students to work together on pairwork activities throughout the course, and to gain confidence in working with a partner as all PET speaking tests are conducted in pairs.
  Pre-teach the names of the colours if these are not already known: *pale green, pink, grey, cream/yellow, blue, purple*; opposite of *pale*: *dark*. Encourage pairs of students to tell the rest of the class how they would arrange the room. Some of the more confident ones could be asked to suggest extra items such as a *desk* or a *picture*.

22 The stimulus material in exercise 21 should lead directly on to the letter-writing task in exercise 22. The beginning of this letter provides the student with plenty of support (see Unit 10 page 109 for an example of Part 3 of the Writing Paper), and only requires the student to produce about 60 words at this stage of the course.
  It is a good idea to teach students the format and conventions of informal letter-writing if they do not already know these. If they are required to write to a friend this means choosing someone's name and not just using *friend*. Make sure your students also know that it is not customary to begin letters with *Hi!* or *Hello* but with *Dear . . .*
  The kind of letter-writing required for the PET will usually be informal and addressed to a friend or relative. So although the address, salutation and endings are not normally tested, it is worth teaching your students the most common, informal endings such as *Love from . . .* and *With best wishes from . . .* (For further examples of letters see Unit 6(7), Unit 7(19) and Unit 9(19).)

◆ *Speaking* (p. 21)

23 Encourage students to produce a few sentences about their photograph. They should concentrate on organising what they want to say so that they work towards linking their ideas and expressing themselves coherently. Point out to them that the ability to draw is certainly never tested, but this is an opportunity to give and to listen to instructions.

◆ *Listening* (p. 22)

24 The tape for this exercise consists of five discrete or separate dialogues, and is introduced at this stage to prepare students for Part 1 of the Listening Paper. On the PET Listening Paper each set of pictures is preceded by a written question to focus the candidate's attention on the specific information to listen for. (Practice for this part of the paper is given on page 122 as an extension exercise to Unit 4.)

Begin by discussing with the class the drawings/photographs and the kinds of context or situation each set of pictures suggests. Students should now be able to supply the vocabulary to describe what they can see in each set of pictures. In question 4 make sure that students understand that the line drawings represent the ground floor plan only.

Play each short recording at least twice. (They are each repeated once on the tape.)

Key: 1 C   2 B   3 D   4 A   5 A

◆ *Know your vocabulary* (p. 23)

25 Key:

26 Checklist:

1 upstairs	6 cupboard	10 elevator*
2 downstairs	7 living room	11 inhabitant
3 bookcase	8 bungalow	12 lavatory
4 kitchen	9 apartment	13 escalator
5 dining room		

*(NB British English: *lift*)

Note: Context and speaker's intention affect the position of word stress. In this list, for example, the words upstairs and downstairs both commonly occur with the stress on the other syllable from that given here.

27 Key: *For sale* means you can buy this property from whoever is selling it and it then becomes yours.

To rent means you can pay a sum of money every week/month in order to live here but the property never belongs to you.

28 Key: The signs (billboards) can be seen outside the house/flat being advertised, usually fixed onto a post in the ground.

Room to let: This is a personal advertisement which can be seen in a newsagent's window, or occasionally in the window of the house where the room is available.

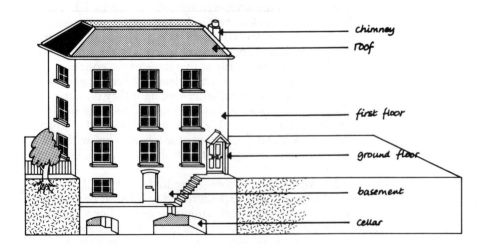

Unit 3 Shopping

◆ Lead-in (p. 24)

2 The tourist exchange rates table can be extended by asking students to collect further examples from banks, tourist offices, newspapers etc. (The list here is taken from a travel agent's window which lists countries alphabetically.) With a younger class of students who may not have travelled abroad it is also a good idea to take into the classroom foreign coins and/or notes to stimulate their interest. The short listening exercise provides further practice in listening to and recording figures.

Key:

Bureau de Change

Rates per £1	We Buy	We Sell
Australian $	2.33	2.14
Austria Sch	16.59	15.21
Belgium Fr.	48.72	44.77
Canada $	2.38	2.21
Finland Mkk	7.62	6.91
France Fr.	8.28	7.63
Germany Dm.	2.36	2.17
Greece Dr.	383.00	358.00
Holland Gld		

3 If students have difficulty in identifying the country of origin, then supply the initial letter. This exercise can also be used for further practice in nationality adjectives if necessary. (*Turkish, Danish, Portuguese, Mexican, Thai, Norwegian.*)

Key: 1F Turkey **2E** Denmark **3D** Portugal
4A Mexico **5B** Thailand **6C** Norway

◆ Speaking (p. 25)

4 The suggestions for different kinds of shops may vary depending on the age and background of your class. The notes on exercise 22 include a list of shops which you may want to exploit early on in the unit so that students begin to familiarise themselves with the relevant vocabulary.

5 This exercise may be quite time-consuming, but once your students are clear what they are required to find out, it could be set as a homework task. In this case you will obviously not have any control over whether they use English or their mother-tongue to find out the information. However, try to ensure that they record the information in English so that the written language produces the spoken practice during classroom feedback.

◆ Writing (p. 25)

6 Before asking students to write a short report, use the suggested model to highlight the following language points: *firstly, finally, lastly, although, but, because, more . . . than.*

Encourage students to keep to the model so that they get maximum practice at this stage from a guided writing exercise. The exercise could be started in class and finished off for homework.

◆ Reading (p. 26)

7 Pre-teach *insistent* (adj.). Here it has the sense of demanding something. Also *just* (adv.), in this context in the sense of 'only'.

If students are interested in markets and familiar with other kinds of markets (bird, flower, jewellery etc.) you might wish to develop this topic further, e.g. by discussion and vocabulary-building or a short written report on a market which the student knows well.

Key: 1 Yes **2** No **3** Yes **4** No **5** Yes

◆ Listening (pp. 26–27)

8 **Key: 1** post office **2** hairdresser
3 police station **4** bank **5** cleaners

9 Make sure that students know the name of each item. As a pre-listening exercise you could ask the students to predict the price of each article! When completing the task encourage students to write the prices using numbers, putting the £ sign before the figure and p (pence) after the figure if there are no pounds.

Key: pencils £3.50; jacket £150.00; camera £30.00; sweater £25.99; tin opener 72p

---

◆ Grammar (pp. 27–28)

10   Point out to your students that zero conditionals are used for giving instructions. They should not confuse this form with the first conditional.

11   Allow for answers which are relevant to the students' own environment, e.g. in some countries you can buy stamps from a newsagent or a tobacconist.

12, 13, 14   All the examples here rely on regular verb forms which should have been practised in Unit 1 (10).

12   Key: 3 . . . to have my car repaired.
4 . . . to have her car cleaned.
5 . . . to have their shoes heeled.

14   Key: *Note*: Possible alternative structures are given in brackets in case students ask whether all these sentences lend themselves to being expressed both ways. In some cases either the active or the passive is the only correct answer.
1 My passport needs renewing. (I need to renew my passport.)
2 Rosa needs to have her photo taken. (Rosa needs her photo taking.)
3 I need to buy a suitcase.
4 Our house needs painting.
5 David needs to phone his brother.
6 Dan's bike needs repairing. (Dan needs to have his bike repaired.)
7 The police need to catch the thief.
8 I need to have my teeth checked. (My teeth need checking.)

◆ Reading (pp. 28–29)

15   Encourage students to scan the advertisements before looking at the questions. Pre-teach *off*. This is a very common way of showing a reduction on the usual price of something.

Key: 1 the chance to buy shampoo for 15p less than normal price
2 Twells plc
3 phone British Gas
4 one day
5 tomatoes (*Note*: Students should recognise that *lb* is the abbreviation for a pound weight (there are 2.2 pounds in 1 kilo). Class 1 – the best grade of tomatoes.)

6 Thomas Cook
7 information about carpets
8 free dry cleaning

◆ Writing (p. 29)

16   Depending on the age of your students you could suggest that they choose a well-known painting (obviously a reproduction!) and in presenting a few written clues ask their partner to try and guess the artist/title of the painting. Otherwise this task works perfectly well as a short productive exercise without the pairwork dimension.

◆ Writing (p. 30)

17   This provides further practice in form-filling. Students may not want to fill in a postcode (Am. Eng. *zipcode*), in which case it is worth training your students always to indicate a nil response to a space on a form by putting a dash to show that they have noted the point.

◆ Listening (p. 30)

18   Pre-teach *gift-wrapped* (adj.): a service (sometimes free of charge in the UK) by which items are wrapped in gift-wrapping paper by the shop where they are bought.
   It might also be worth discussing the concept of a *shopping precinct* (often called a *shopping mall*) if your students are not familiar with the idea of a number of shops under one roof. These precincts can sometimes be very elaborate – with plants, fountains, cafés and recreation areas.
   Make sure your students know how to read the grid, i.e. both vertically and horizontally, before they complete it.

Key:

Shopping Precinct			
LEVEL	1	2	3
cafe/bar			✔
shoes	✔		
dried flowers		✔	
gardens			✔
souvenirs/gifts		✔	
clothes	✔		
postal service		✔	
chocolate		✔	

◆ *Speaking and Writing* (p. 30)

19, 20, 21 Even if your students do not live in a town, most of them will be familiar with the nearest town in their area. Before embarking on this section, however, you should discuss with your class what they understand by *facilities* (even though the word falls outside the productive level for PET). The word can be used quite loosely when talking about a town to include (in addition to shops) things like cinemas, theatres, libraries, parks and gardens, restaurants and bars, sports amenities and even public toilets! In exercise 19 the word *services* is used to cover this range of possibilities.

◆ *Know your vocabulary* (p. 31)

22 Depending on the age of your students they may enjoy trying to identify goods in the shop windows prior to labelling each shop. If you want to give your students the names of the shops to help them with this task, you can write the following list on the board. (Make sure you don't write the list in the order given in the Key!)

bakery   grocer
butchers   jewellers
chemist   newsagents
giftshop   supermarket
greengrocer   sweetshop

Key:

23   Key: **1** Ask students to work out the collection time depending on what time they do this exercise.
2 This sign is used to indicate that something mechanical is broken.
3 A French term (Am. Eng. *General Delivery*) used as an address so that a letter will be held at a specific post office until it is collected.

24   Checklist:

1 electricity	5 operator	9 shop assistant
2 self-service	6 borrow	10 customer
3 souvenir	7 weight	11 account
4 telephone	8 market	12 dial

Unit 4 Food and Drink

◆ Lead-in (p. 32)

1 Use the sweet jars for a quick guessing game and oral practice in producing letters and numbers.

Key: A and 66.

2 The shopping bag can be used as a way of brainstorming all the different food names that students may already know. Obviously students are not expected to imagine what is in the bag from an English shopper's point of view and the things that can partly be seen – lemon, bananas, apple, green beans, bottle of wine, spaghetti, bread, tea and orange juice – are not necessarily culture-specific. During the course of the unit students will encounter most of the vocabulary for this topic area that falls within the productive level for PET. However, there are also opportunities in this unit for students to exploit the different foods of their own countries (exercises 7, 8 and 18), and whilst the names of dishes are not always translatable, students should be encouraged to know the names of the basic ingredients in English for these dishes.

◆ Listening (p. 33)

3 The shopping bill is from an English supermarket. It might be interesting to ask students to bring in a similar receipt for comparison of prices. The less obvious abbreviations on the bill are explained in the note below for your information only – students do not need to learn these, but should recognise *lb* from Unit 3(15). Before playing the tape make sure your students have studied the bill, understand the items listed, and know how to record the prices they hear.

Note: @ is a symbol meaning 'at', commonly used when giving a price for a particular quantity. *Bal* is an abbreviation for 'balance'.

Key: 12 items; Total bill £7.66; No – she received 34p change.

4 **Key:**

```
        J SAINSBURY PLC
            BATH
     TELEPHONE NO. 0225 444737

                              £
   SQUEEZY HONEY          0.72
   JS HALF FAT MILK       0.26
   JS CORNFLAKES          0.82
   JS HOVIS LOAF          0.53
   LEMON TEA BAGS         1.19
   NEW POTATOES           0.68
   JS FILTER COFFEE       0.99
 BANANAS
 1.40 lb @ £0.56/lb       0.78
 TOMATOES
 0.18 lb @ £0.95/lb       0.17
 CARROTS
 1.20 lb @ £0.29/lb       0.35
   HALF CUCUMBER          0.38
   CAULIFLOWER            0.79

   BAL DUE                7.66

 CASH                     8.00
 CHANGE                   0.34


   005 17 141 6008 10:01 23MAR96

   THANK YOU FOR YOUR CUSTOM
   PLEASE RETAIN THIS RECEIPT IN
      CASE OF ANY QUERY
```

◆ Reading (pp. 33–34)

5, 6 It is not necessary for students to learn everything on this menu. They should, however, be able to recognise the different courses described on the menu – helped here by the fact that the restaurant uses ✽✽✽✽✽✽✽✽ to separate the starters, main courses, vegetables and desserts (sweets). Notice also that the steaks are described in terms of the cut of the meat (fillet, sirloin and T-Bone) and weight (7oz, 8oz and 16oz). Students are expected to know that *oz* is short for ounce. There are 16 ounces in a pound (*lb*) and 8oz is equal to approximately 225g.

6 **Key:** 4 starters.
Chicken with bacon (NB seasoning is a mixture of herbs and spices), plaice (a flat fish), steak, ham omelette. Coffee is included in the price.
Meal cost £17.50.

◆ Writing (p. 35)

7 Before beginning this exercise you may like to have a short discussion on what your students regard as a 'typical menu' for their country. This exercise can be done as pairwork or homework depending on how much 'research' is needed on prices! If there is time, get the class to exchange their sample menus for further discussion.

◆ Speaking (p. 35)

8 The responses to these three questions can be exploited further as a short written exercise once the students have collected their information. You may want to treat it as a guided writing exercise, in which case you will need to give students a framework for the task. The following suggestion reinforces a previous example from Unit 3(6): 'My favourite food and drink are . . . and my favourite meal is . . . Other people in my class, however, like . . . although . . .'

◆ Reading (p. 35)

9 Key: 1 The ability to recognise the writer's purpose and equally why someone would read a text is tested in Part 4 of the Reading Paper. Once students have read the text, ask them to guess where it might come from and what kind of clues can give them help. For example, the use of 'we', the style and tone – almost spoken English in parts – 'It was fantastic!', 'why not come here?', the short form of verbs e.g. 'we'd', 'haven't', 'you'd', 'there's' all suggest the informality of a letter to a member of one's family or a close friend. In the actual PET students are presented with this task in the form of a multiple-choice question. The 'detective work' described above, however, can be applied to all the reading extracts in this book and even to single sentences as a way of training students to identify sources.
2 The same process applies to identifying a writer's intention, and in the PET this question is also presented as a multiple-choice item. The question here is open-ended so that there is more than one possible answer, e.g. describing a good holiday/an excellent meal/recommending the people to whom the letter is addressed to take their holiday in the same place.
3 The writer likes the food, the friendly waiters and the fact that the restaurant is not expensive. Tell your students to concentrate on a brief answer which picks out the relevant points.
4 The writer is planning to make coconut ice-cream.
5 That the readers should go to the same place for their holiday if they can/if they haven't already planned where to go.
6 To find out about a friend's holiday.

◆ Listening (p. 36)

10 Before listening to the tape make sure your students know the names of the various eating places:
1 restaurant; 2 café 3 snack bar (here open-air)
4 self-service restaurant; 5 bar/pub.

Key: A 3   B 1   C 4   D 2   E 5

◆ Grammar (pp. 36–37)

11, 12, 13, 14 This section covers the positions of adverbs at an elementary level. The main teaching point is to alert students to the fact that adverbs in an English sentence are not (or are very seldom) placed between a verb and 'its object. As well as students needing to know about adverbial position for written purposes, they may find this grammatical point is actively tested in Part 1 of the Writing Paper.
In the key, the answer given is the most obvious one. It is possible to come across variations at a more sophisticated level such as in exercise 11, 2 'Can I, too, come to the café?' but these variations are not included here.

11 Key: 1 Michael did his homework very well.
2 Can I come to the café too?

12 Key: 1 I like reading cookery books very much.
or (less likely) I very much like reading cookery books.
2 I don't like carrying heavy bags of shopping much.
or (less likely) I don't much like carrying heavy bags of shopping.

13 Key: 1 We often do our shopping on a Saturday.
2 I am always happy to cook for my friends.

14 Key: 1 I have always bought fresh eggs from my local farm.
2 I have never liked drinking coffee late at night.
3 If you keep taking the cake out of the oven it will never rise.
4 Have you ever eaten raw fish?

◆ Reading (p. 38)

15 The purpose behind this task is to encourage students to skim through a text without feeling the need to read every single word. In that sense, the task is very different from the one they will have encountered in exercise 9. When it comes to preparing your students for Part 3 of the Reading Paper, you should encourage them to read the questions before the text, as in this way they will scan the text looking for an answer to a particular question. At this stage of the course, however, you should tackle this as a class exercise (and allow for detailed reading) with the students working in pairs for support. Make sure, though, that the students realise, for example, that question 3 can be answered without reference to the description of the Rajpoot's food, and that in any case most of the vocabulary in the advertisement falls outside PET level. So the skill lies in disregarding what is not relevant to the question!

Key: **1** 7 days   **2** The Four Seasons   **3** No
4 The New York Pizza Co.   **5** The Cricketers

◆ *Speaking and Writing (p. 39)*

16, 17   This section enables students to revise the adverbs of frequency practised in the Grammar section (exercises 11–14).

Make sure your students copy down the questions for their own questionnaires correctly. You may want to adapt the questions slightly if there is a popular snack food which is more relevant to your students than the ones listed here. The same criterion will apply to the suggested names of fizzy drinks. This issue of food and health is dealt with in more detail in Unit 5, but the connection is made here between snack foods and unhealthy eating habits. It would not be appropriate to labour this point, and different nationalities will react differently to this assumption anyway. The main objectives are to exploit the section for its speaking and writing skills.

If you don't want to use class time for your students to find out this information then ask them to do it for homework, on the understanding of course that they record the answers in English, even if they ask the questions in their mother tongue. In order to get a clear indication of people's habits for the report writing task (exercise 17) they will need to convert the answers into scores.

If you feel that some of the students would benefit from another guided writing task, then you can supply an optional framework for the report. Although the suggestions below refer to the number of each question, students should be asked to write the report as one piece of continuous prose. For example:
1 Most/All/Half/50% of the students I asked think that they eat too much . . .
Not many/Only two think that . . .
2 Some people say that they eat snacks in between meals like . . .
Other people eat things like . . .
3 Some people drink . . . but others drink . . .
4 Most of them/All of them enjoy eating foods like . . .

◆ *Speaking and Writing (p. 39)*

18   This writing task is more structured than the one that follows (exercise 19) in that there is a model for students to use if they wish. Encourage students to choose a simple recipe. If some of the class are less interested in food than others, allow for a brain-storming session to provide ideas, or ask students to bring recipes

to the lesson from home/family (which may then need to be translated).

Students will see from the model that they are using the infinitive of the verb without *to* in order to give instructions, and this use of the verb is highlighted later in the course in Unit 8 (11, 12). Encourage the class to use a dictionary to find out any additional vocabulary that they are likely to need for this task. There is no need for students to learn words which fall outside the level in this recipe, e.g. *de-seed*, *strip*, although they can expect to encounter words like *slice* and *peel* for receptive purposes, and should know words like *mix*, *cut*, *fry*, *boil* and *grill*.

With a young class you could treat the checking exercise as a game, awarding points to the pairs who spot mistakes in a recipe – provided they can correct the mistakes!

◆ *Writing (p. 40)*

19   Ideally this letter should be set as a homework task as a follow-up to the guided writing tasks (exercises 7 and 18). This time, however, the support material lies in the advertisement details for the competition, and the framework for the letter is supplied in the form of the points which the letter has to include. It is important that the students realise that this task begins to approximate to what they can expect in Part 3 of the Writing Paper. (It is unlikely that the stimulus material would be so detailed in the PET.) Encourage your students to aim for simple accurate sentences, and to check their work for any mistakes before they hand it in.

◆ *Know your vocabulary (p. 41)*

20   Key: **1** 20th January 1996 **2** No. 4 **3** 19.07/ seven minutes past seven **4** 6 (C = cover, i.e. individual table setting) **5** £9.16 **6** £76.30 **7** Not normally, as a service charge has been added to the bill

Note: Service charges can vary. They can range from 10% – 15%. In some cases there is no service charge.

21   Key: **1** give/bring **2** take **3** fetch **4** bring **5** show **6** send

Note: Other answers are possible, but less likely.

22   The list here may introduce new vocabulary as well as revise vocabulary that has already cropped up during the unit. Students can always add to the list if they come across new words which they want to learn.

Checklist:

1 potatoes	5 pudding	9 thirsty	13 chicken
2 tomatoes	6 steak	10 salad	14 toast
3 cauliflower	7 sandwich	11 menu	15 steamed
4 honey	8 hungry	12 cabbage	

Unit 5 Health and Lifestyles

◆ Lead-in (p. 42)

1 The jokes here are used as a lead-in to the first section of the unit, which focuses on parts of the body and goes on to include health, visiting a doctor, and hospitals. If you are teaching a multi-lingual class there is a danger that the jokes may fall flat if you have to rely on too much translation. You must judge how far you can exploit the material. You may need to pre-teach the meaning of *ignore*. If the jokes go down well you could try including these as well:

'Doctor, doctor, I keep thinking I'm a dog.'
'Get on the couch please.'
'But I'm not allowed on the couch!'

'Doctor, doctor, I keep thinking I'm a pair of curtains.'
'Pull yourself together, man!'

2 Some of the vocabulary for this exercise is listed here marked with the main stresses, to enable you to give students specific pronunciation practice.

stŏmach (*Note*: When referring to a pain in this part of the body below the waist, people, and especially children, often use the word 'tummy'.)

fĭnger   knĕe (silent *k*)
hĕart   thŭmb (silent *b*)

Key:

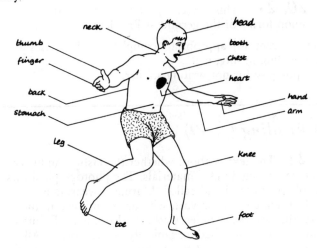

◆ Reading (p. 43)

3, 4, 5 When students have written down the things they do to look and feel good, ask them to put their suggestions to one side, and then divide the class into small groups.

Pre-teach *skin* and *spotty*. After students have written their five questions on the text, exchanged them and checked their answers, they could then compare their suggestions with those of the article.

Note: Point out to students the way the writer uses *Do* and *Don't* for giving emphatic advice.

Key: This text is taken from an article in a women's magazine.
The writer is trying to persuade people that a healthy diet and healthy lifestyle enable one to feel and look fit.

◆ Speaking (p. 44)

6, 7 Make sure that you provide the students with clear models which ensure that they practise the contrast between the present perfect tense (exercise 6) and the simple past (exercise 7). One way to do this would be to ask members of the class to put the questions to **you** (so that you act as the role model), getting them to note the structures **you** use to reply.

8, 9 Monitor what the students are writing by periodically getting pairs of students to read their questions out aloud.

◆ Listening (p. 45)

10 Before you play the tape ask the students to look at the doctor's note, and to predict what kind of answers they can expect to write in the gaps (1–4). Then play the tape, suggesting that on the first playing they just listen. This task is relatively easy, and should be regarded as a way of giving students confidence to deal with Part 3 of the Listening Paper.

Key: 1 Jones   2 frying pan   3 (hot) oil   4 right leg

◆ Listening (p. 45)

11 There is vocabulary in this listening extract which falls outside the PET level. You should warn the class that they can expect to hear some unfamiliar words, but that coping with the task does not depend on understanding these words. The words outside the productive level are *compound*, *sense*, and *shift*.

Before you play the tape, make sure that the students have read the statements and understand the task.

Pre-teach *might*, used here and in exercise 13 (Maya's Day) to suggest possibility.

Key: I go shopping every day.   M
I don't have to cook for myself.   R
At weekends I like to sleep.   R
I'm a nurse.   R
I'm a teacher.   M
I always have a rest in the middle of the day.   M
I don't do much shopping.   R
My working days are never the same.   R
I work a very long day.   M
At weekends I sometimes go to the coast.   M

◆ Reading (p. 46)

12, 13 Use these photographs and questions as a
prediction exercise before moving on to exercise 13. You
could also ask students to discuss their own daily
routine. Alternatively, you could ask them to read about
Joe and Maya first and then contrast what they have
read with their own experience.

Joe: Born in London
Maya: Dutch, lives in Amsterdam

◆ Speaking and Writing (p. 46)

14 Two tasks are included here. If you are teaching
a monolingual, monocultural class the interview exercise
may not stimulate students' interest, in which case you
should direct them to base their speaking practice on the
photographs. The writing task requires students to
identify with one or both characters. As these two
photos are anonymous, students can be asked to give
each person a name and to suggest where they might live
before writing. Some students may wish to keep very
closely to the structural patterns used by Joe and Maya,
but in any case they should be encouraged to use *might*
in context.

◆ Listening (p. 47)

15 The four extracts on the tape introduce students
to the language structures they need to learn in order to
tackle the role play in exercise 16. After they have
finished the exercise, play the tape again, this time
pausing after each extract in order to highlight the
structures.
    For example in extract 1: *I'd like to make an
appointment . . .*
2 *Take two tablets three times a day . . .* This structure
will be primarily receptive, but is included here for
students to familiarise themselves with the way in which
instructions for taking medicine (here tablets) are given.
3 *. . . can I see a doctor please?* The urgent tone and
abrupt structure reflect the emergency of the situation.
4 *Here . . . right here . . . and it's worse when . . .*
Obviously in a real-life situation we indicate the position

of a pain by pointing to its location.
Key: 1 D   **2** C   **3** C   **4** B

◆ Speaking (p. 47)

16 If necessary pre-teach *receptionist*, *aspirin* and
fever (all productive). Remind students that we express
sympathy through the tone of our voice with the
intention of sharing a person's feelings. We use phrases
such as 'Oh dear', and make suggestions: 'Why don't
you go to bed . . .', 'You might feel better after a day in
bed'. Allow time for students to practise all the role
plays and to listen to some of this pairwork in class.

◆ Grammar (p. 48)

17 Explain 'verb base'; some students may have
learnt to talk about the 'infinitive without *to*'.

18 Key: 1 e.g. . . . is bad for your health/can be
very boring. (but accept any appropriate completion)
2 Eating
3 (accept any appropriate completion)
4 Reading

19 Key: 1 . . . old frightens many people.
or. . . old is frightening for many people.
2 . . . is bad for one's health.
3 . . . weight is (very) difficult for some people.
4 . . . the dentist makes some people nervous. (*Note*: to
    make someone nervous)
5 . . . too much fatty food is bad for your heart.

20, 21 This exercise practises some of the
common forms of the gerund at PET level.

Key: Accept any appropriate completion which uses a
verb ending in -*ing*, e.g.
1 I apologise for not writing sooner.

◆ Reading (p. 49)

22 The text is about whether the fashion industry
will start using natural materials. The photograph shows
people (from the band called 'Marines') wearing a
T-shirt made by Reactivart, who are mentioned in the
text. (In case your students ask, the Reactivart T-shirt is
made from unbleached, organically grown cotton. All the
money from the sale of the T-shirts goes directly into the
Green Ideas Trust which funds workshops in the UK to
teach young people to become more environmentally
aware.)

23 All the missing words are used here as
connectors to link ideas together. Students should work
independently on this exercise.

Ensure the class reads the text before you put the following words on the board. Make sure you jumble the words, as they are listed here in the order in which they occur in the text!

Key: when, that, but, because, and, whether

◆ *Writing (p. 49)*

24 Activate vocabulary for this exercise by discussing in class what is happening in each picture; or if you want to set this exercise for homework encourage students to use their dictionaries. You can give extra support by using the first picture as a class exercise to make sure the students use the simple/continuous past tense for their letters.

◆ *Know your vocabulary (pp. 50–51)*

25 Depending on your class you may need to treat this brief exercise on world religions very sensitively. It should be presented for vocabulary purposes only, pointing out to students that they should be able to recognise these words which affect people's lifestyles. The text material is taken from an article in *The Indy* called 'Who am I and what am I doing here?' (*The Indy* is a newspaper published in the UK for young people.)

Key: **A5   B3   C1   D2   E4**

26 Key:

27 *Note: Jab* is informal.

28 **Checklist:**

Phonetic transcriptions are included to clarify pronunciation of certain words.

1 cough /kɒf/   6 blood
2 wound /wuːnd/   7 ache /eɪk/
3 hygiene   8 specialist
4 dead   9 surgeon /'sɜːdʒən/
5 die   10 death

29 *What's up with you?* This is a very common, informal way of asking someone what is wrong or what is the matter with them – sometimes reduced to just the two words: *What's up?*

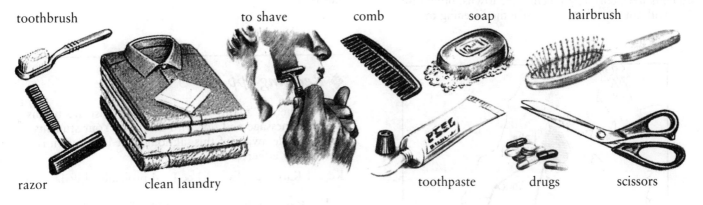

toothbrush   to shave   comb   soap   hairbrush

razor   clean laundry   toothpaste   drugs   scissors

Unit 6 Holidays and Travel

◆ Lead-in (p. 52)

1, 2   With a young class you might wish to turn this exercise into more of a game, giving them an atlas or a globe and making the task competitive.

The main stresses are marked for pronunciation practice.

1 **Key: A** Perú **B** Finland **C** Kenya **D** Wales
E Austria **F** Sri Lanka

2 **Key: A** Lima   **B** Helsinki   **C** Nairobi
D Cardiff **E** Vienna **F** Colombo

(The countries and capitals not represented visually are:

Egypt/Cairo; The Czech Republic/Prague

The Philippines/Manila; Canada/Ottawa)

◆ Listening (p. 52)

3   Some of your students may be able to name some of these places, e.g. London. You can try putting the names on the board – Bristol, Brighton, Oxford, Cambridge, Birmingham, London – and encourage guessing!

Make sure that before you play the tape all the students have correctly labelled the towns, otherwise they will not be able to complete the listening task.

4 **Key:**

◆ Reading (p. 53)

5   Pre-teach *double* (for two people) and *single* (for one person) in the context of accommodation. It is also worth pointing out that UK prices usually include breakfast.

Encourage students to scan a text for relevant information and not to worry if they don't understand every word. If you want to exploit a text for specific test preparation, train your students to read the questions before reading the text, as this will help them to focus on the specific information they are looking for.

Key: 1 Yes **2** No **3** Yes **4** Yes **5** No

6 **Key:** Ted and Amy would be likely to choose the Grasmere first as it is small and the price is right; the Washington would probably be their second choice.

◆ Writing (p. 54)

7   This letter is set out to show students a customary layout. Although it is unlikely that in the PET they will be required to supply an address on a letter, they should know the opening and closing conventions for formal and informal letter-writing. (Informal closing conventions are included in exercise 8.) A formal letter which begins with *Dear Sir/Madam* should conclude with *Yours faithfully*; a formal letter which addresses the person by name should conclude with *Yours sincerely*.

Key: Dear, would, single, for, from, to, with, or, faithfully

◆ Reading (pp. 54–55)

8   There is a convention whereby a postcard begins with the message and not with *Dear . . .* Your students can be made aware of this, although the convention is not strictly adhered to.

Key: 1 Katy **2** Olly   **3** J & J   **4** probably H & D

9 **Key: 1** Olly **2** Katy **3** H + D **4** J & J

10   Before students do this writing task they should look carefully at the written examples in exercise 8, the simple phrases the writers use to describe where they are and what they are doing, and how they end their messages. You might like to set the postcard task for homework. It is important that the students write to someone specific as this generally helps to convey a more genuine and personal message. There is no reason why both postcards cannot be used, but you could use the picture which the students don't choose as a revision exercise at a later date.

♦ *Speaking (p. 56)*

11   Pre-teach *full board* (all meals included), *half-board* (breakfast and either lunch or dinner – usually the evening meal). Stars ** beside a hotel rate a hotel's facilities – the more stars the better the hotel. *Supplement* – in this context a noun meaning an extra charge.

You will also need to discuss exchange rates so that students can work out prices, and this might be something you ask them to do prior to the lesson if you are teaching a multi-lingual class.

It is not necessary for students to understand everything in order to work through this oral task. Allow time in class to listen to some of the pair work.

♦ *Grammar (pp. 57–58)*

12   Grammar is given more prominence in this unit, as students are now halfway through the course and should be finding it easier to absorb more material by building on what they have already learnt.

Sentence **2** is more natural because **what** is grown is more important than who grows it.

The explanations accompanying the uses of the passive are deliberately simple, designed to help students recognise the patterns and to cope with Part 1 of the Writing Paper, in which they may be required to rewrite simple passive sentences as active and vice versa.

Make sure students understand the basic rule by highlighting it on the board before they do exercise 13.

The tense in the active form remains the same as the tense in the passive form.

In the passive the verb *to be* is put into the appropriate tense followed by the past participle.

13   **Key: 1** . . . booked the flight.
2 . . . are made in the USA.
3 . . . was stopped by the customs officer as he got off the plane.
4 . . . is being drunk more than ever nowadays.
5 . . . was brought into England in the seventeenth century.
6 . . . are being made by scientists all the time.
7 . . . was broken into yesterday.
8 . . . was delayed by a heavy snowfall.
9 . . . are sold in the market. (unnecessary to add *by people*)
10 . . . is planning a new Hong Kong airport for next century.

14   The following notes explain the simple uses of the relative pronoun which you should discuss with your class before moving on to the exercise.

who/that	– used to refer to people
whom	– the object form of *who* and not often used in spoken English
whose	– used to refer to possession of people or things
which/that	– used to refer to things

Relative pronouns can replace subjects/objects of verbs, as well as acting as connectors to link sentences together. The following example illustrates both these uses in the one sentence.

What is the name of the hotel? You stayed there last year.
What is the name of the hotel which *you stayed at last year?*

A relative pronoun can be omitted from a relative clause if it is not the subject of the clause. In the example it is not wrong to include *which*, but it can perfectly well be left out.

The holiday (which) I went on this year was the best I've ever had.

Key: 1 none necessary
2 which/that
3 Who
4 whose
5 none necessary
6 which/that

♦ *Listening (p. 58)*

15   This exercise can be approached by asking students in the first instance to guess where they would come across the various notices.

1 a notice in a hotel bedrom
2 a card issued by hotel reception
3 information in a hotel bedroom
4 the leaflet is an advertisement for taking your bike on a train
5 advertisement for student coach travel

You might want to play the tape right the way through, or pause after each extract so that students can fill in the information.

Key: 1 241; 19th; 2.30 (14.30); hairdryer broken/ hairdryer not working/broken hairdryer
2 Mr King; 23rd; 25th; double; £62; 33
3 Oct(ober) 6(th); circle or tick 3 and 4 (cloud and umbrella); 8; 46
4 7.10; 19.48
5 2/two photos; college; £5

♦ *Reading (p. 59)*

16   Quickly use the opening questions to set the context for the reading task.

Pre-teach *valid/validity*. For documents like passports or tickets it means they can be used and will be accepted by people in authority. Also *prior* – before; *rug* – here used with the meaning of blanket; *pillow* (productive) – a cushion for resting your head; YMCA – Young Men's Christian Association, similar to a youth hostel and caters for both sexes.

There is some (but not much) redundancy in this text, so students need to read the whole text carefully. Underlining parts of a text sometimes helps to focus on the relevant sections.

Key: 1 Yes 2 Yes 3 No 4 No 5 given 6 No. 7 No 8 Yes

◆ Writing (p. 60)

17 This Fact Sheet can be completed individually or in pairs. If this task is difficult to set for homework because your class doesn't have easy access to the information in a library, you could bring textbooks into the classroom. Don't worry if the textbooks are not in English, as you can check orally on the numbers which they look up, and they will have to translate the notes they write under 'Climate'. If there is time, the completed Fact Sheet could be used as a stimulus for writing a short report, maybe comparing/contrasting two or three countries or their own country with another example.

Key:

COUNTRY (language)	POPULATION	CAPITAL	CURRENCY	CLIMATE
UNITED KINGDOM English	57,750,000	London	sterling	cool, rainy, fog in winter
SPAIN Spanish	39,322,000	Madrid	peseta	sunny in the south but cold in the north
ITALY Italian	57,747,000	Rome	lira	cold winters in the north, hot and dry in summer
BELGIUM 1) French 2) Flemish	10,022,000	Brussels	franc	cool and wet
JAPAN Japanese	124,044,000	Tokyo	yen	Cold winters in the north, hot summers, monsoon rains May – Sept.
TURKEY Turkish	60,777,000	Ankara	lira	Cold in the mountains, hot and dry in summer.

◆ Know your vocabulary (p. 61)

18
January	April	July	October
February	May	August	November
March	June	September	December

19 Spring Summer Autumn Winter

20 Checklist:

1 scenery 5 lightning 9 frontier
2 zero 6 shade 10 earth
3 temperature 7 terminal 11 stewardess
4 thunder 8 immigration 12 harbour

21

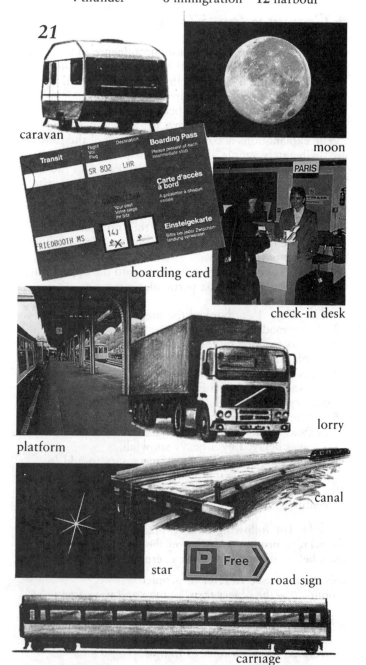

caravan

moon

boarding card

check-in desk

platform

lorry

star

canal

road sign

carriage

Unit 7 Education

This unit focuses on education, but also covers the vocabulary (exercises 26–28) and topics relevant to politics and language learning.

◆ Lead-in (p. 62)

1 This exercise can be done by the students tracing the coloured threads from speech bubble to face. If you want to revise nationality adjectives, you could also ask students to guess country of origin for each person. The key includes some suggestions, but obviously there could be many alternatives.

Pre-teach *Reuters* – the name of an international news agency.

Key:

Boris – Polish; Keiko – Japanese; Olaf – Norwegian; Yunus – Turkish; Marta – Brazilian; Xavier – French; Ruth – Australian; Nikola – German

2 This pairwork practice highlights the contrast between the present simple and present progressive tenses in a way which students may not have encountered before. Use it for repetition of the two structures before you elicit the patterns which students are going write to in the boxes. They will probably have learnt that the present simple is used for routine, habitual actions, e.g. *I get up at six thirty every day*. The contrast here, however, is between the finite nature of being a student (i.e. you are in the process of doing or completing something) and the more permanent nature of a regular job. It is a form which the students can expect to use in the first section of the oral (general conversation) when they are asked to give essential details about themselves.

3 If all your students go to the same school it might be better to omit this exercise, though if you feel students need to practise the structures then you could

Yunus – I work for Reuters – I'm a translator.

Ruth – I teach English in Nepal.

Keiko – I'm in my first year in University.

Olaf – I'm training to be a hotel manager.

Boris – I'm at music college.

Marta – I'm studying medicine.

Nikola – I'm doing a language course in the USA.

Xavier – I'm in my last year at school.

turn it into a pairwork role play, with one person taking the part of one of the people in the photographs.

◆ Reading (p. 63)

4 Encourage your students to scan the text for its general meaning (gist), and to delay reading it intensively until exercise 5.

This article is taken from the newspaper *The Indy*.

Before moving on to exercise 5 you may wish to pre-teach *wander* – to walk around in a casual way; *chop* – to cut something into pieces using an axe or a knife; *odd jobs* – varied, casual work; *provide* – to make something available; *traveller* – in this context a Romany or gypsy.

5 It is very important that students read the questions prior to concentrating on the passage, and that you draw their attention to the fact that these questions are to be answered using only a few words. This is designed to prepare them for PET Question 5 sub-questions 3 and 4, which do not need to be answered in full sentences. The ability to pick out the relevant part of the text (not to copy out chunks) is the important skill.

Key: 1 C   2 D

◆ Grammar (pp. 64–66)

6 **Key:** 1 in   2 for   3 in   4 in   5 with   6 for

7 **Key:** at; at; to; On; in/at; at; at; During

8 **Key:**

1 across, to	✓	☐
2 along, by	✓	☐
3 near	☐	✓
4 down	☐	✓
5 into	☐	✓
6 up to, to	✓	☐
7 off, down	☐	✓

9, 10 By way of introduction ask students what they already know about *must*. Explain that *must* has no infinitive, no participles, no past tense and no third person -*s* in the singular. The explanations are deliberately simplified to correspond to what a student can be expected to know at PET level. Pre-teach *obligation*. Point out that *must* and *have to* are very similar in meaning, but if we want to ask a question about obligation in the past we would use *have to*, for example: *Did you* have to *study Latin at school?*

11 Make sure that students know that *ought* is pronounced /ɔːt/.

12 Check that students understand the main difference between *must* and *have to*, which is reinforced again in exercise 13, item 2.

13 Allow time to discuss the alternative answers in this exercise, and encourage students to explain why they think one answer is more appropriate than another. This discussion should help students to realise that modal verbs and their uses are quite complex.

Key: The most suitable answer is listed first.
1 have to (although *must* could also be right if we are thinking of a personal context and not a rule of law)
2 should/ought to (*must* could be right if the person wants to give an order, e.g. a parent telling a child to do something)
3 must
4 shouldn't/oughtn't to (*mustn't* if you intend giving very strong advice)
5 must (*should/ought to* – if you are offering advice)
6 have to (*must* is acceptable but has less idea of external regulation/*don't have to* – if one wants to express no obligation)
7 shouldn't/oughtn't to/mustn't
8 should/ought to
9 have to/must
10 don't have to

◆ Speaking and Writing (p. 66)

14 If your students have left school, this task should draw on their past experience. Otherwise students can relate it to their present environment. The exercise caters for this by giving the alternatives *is/was* in questions 1–4. Questions 5 and 6 are of a general nature.

Pre-teach *CDT* – craft, design and technology; *Home Economics* – the study of food and nutrition; *English* – both language and literature; *compulsory* – something you **have to do**, you have no choice (link this with *obligation*, pre-taught in exercise 9).

15 If your students are going to write a report it should be brief, and the main emphasis should be on accuracy. This exercise is very similar to other written tasks covered in previous units. It can be discussed and prepared in class, and then written up for homework.

◆ Listening (p. 67)

16 Check that students understand the advertisement before they look at Mr Yacoub's notes. Remind students before you play the tape that they should fill in their answers using a few words – they do do not need to write complete sentences.

Key: 1 9.30–12.30 and 2.30/14.30–5.30/17.30, or 6 hours' teaching a day
2 no more/never more than eight/8
3 morning or afternoon only (accept answers which just refer to the times of either the morning or afternoon classes)
4 with a family
in a student hostel

◆ Writing (p. 68)

17 Pre-teach *tear, tore, torn.* (Note the pronunciation of the verb /tɛə/, and the noun connected with crying which is spelt the same way but pronounced /tɪə/.)

Key: tennis and any other appropriate activity e.g. painting, swimming etc.
accommodation
drinks
transport
entertainment

18 The kinds of questions students would need to ask: the dates, the cost, what the programme includes, whether the accommodation is in single or double rooms, how they can apply etc.

19 The letter does not include a space for students to include their own address as this is not required in the PET. However, there is nothing to stop you asking students to use their own address or to invent one. If it is a UK address, remember the house number precedes the name of the street. Remind students that they should now know how to end (and spell) a formal letter which begins *Dear Sir/Madam*. (See notes on Unit 6, exercise 7.) This task could be set for homework.

◆ Reading (pp. 68–69)

20 This section brings together some of the vocabulary which students need for PET. Although there is no specific link between the items the topics are loosely related under the unit title, 'Education'.

Key: A5 B3 C1 D2 E4

You can if you wish ask students to guess where they might read these extracts. A – a newspaper, B – an advertisement, C – a notice in a library, D – a leaflet, E – a student accommodation guide.

◆ Writing (p. 69)

21 This exercise familiarises students with additional relevant vocabulary: *to vote* and *election*, both of which are included in the PET productive list. Some students may be more politically interested and aware than others, in which case they will find the task easier than others. Tell them that one or two sentences are enough. You may want to do this exercise as a class discussion, with students making suggestions as to what 'busy' means in term of voting, i.e. many people turning out to vote. In different countries voting takes place on different days. In the UK for example it is never at a weekend but usually on a Thursday. In other countries it is always at a weekend.

In the second example 'at the top' would on a national basis refer to the people at the top of the central political hierarchy, i.e. people in power – president, prime minister, minister. However, the headline could be interpreted in a more local context i.e. mayor, councillor.

◆ Speaking (p. 70)

22 You might choose to begin this activity by telling the class very briefly about your own experience of starting school. Ask the students to put these questions to you before they work with their partner.

23 The children in the photograph (taken in the primary department of an international school in Switzerland) are engaged in a variety of activities – reading, writing, measuring, weighing, sorting shapes and colours etc. They appear to be about five or six years old.

This speaking activity lends itself to follow-up in the form of a short written task based around one's first day at school. This could be set for homework if appropriate.

◆ Listening (p. 70)

24 Allow time for feedback before moving on to exercise 25. You could put some of the students' suggestions on the board (e.g. *Sorry?*, which is very common, and said with a rising tone) so they can check whether they correspond to what they are going to hear, and also to see if they can extend the list.

25 Make sure everyone understands the pictures, and the fact that they have to write down a sentence from each listening extract. Ask the class to identify the scene/context of each picture before they listen.

Key: 1 I beg your pardon?
2 Excuse me, please. What does 'copy' mean?
3 What is it called?
4 How do you say this word?
5 I don't understand. Can you say that again more slowly please?

◆ *Know your vocabulary* (p. 71)

26 Key:

pupil

queen

king

students   lecturer   old-age pensioner

president

Note: The king is King Taufa'ahan Tupon IV of Tonga, pictured here with his queen after their coronation ceremony. (On the left is the Crown Prince.)
The president is President Vaclav Havel of The Czech Republic.

27 Key:

> When a country has **peace** or is at **peace** it is not involved in a war.

> A **Prime Minister** is the leader of the government of a country.

> A **war** is a period of fighting between countries or states when weapons are used and lots of people get killed.

> **1 politics** refers to the actions or activities which people use to achieve power in a country, society, or organiziation or which ensure that power is used in a particular way.
> **2** Someone's **politics** are their beliefs about how a country ought to be governed.

> **6** A **state** is **6.1** a country, usually when it is considered in terms of its political organization and structure. ...**6.2** one of the the areas or divisions in a country such as the USA or Australia.

28 Checklist:

1 examination
2 government
3 socialist
4 communist
5 conservative
6 primary
7 secondary
8 professional
9 professor
10 translate
11 fail
12 pass
13 term (Am. Eng. semester)
14 pronounce
15 certificate

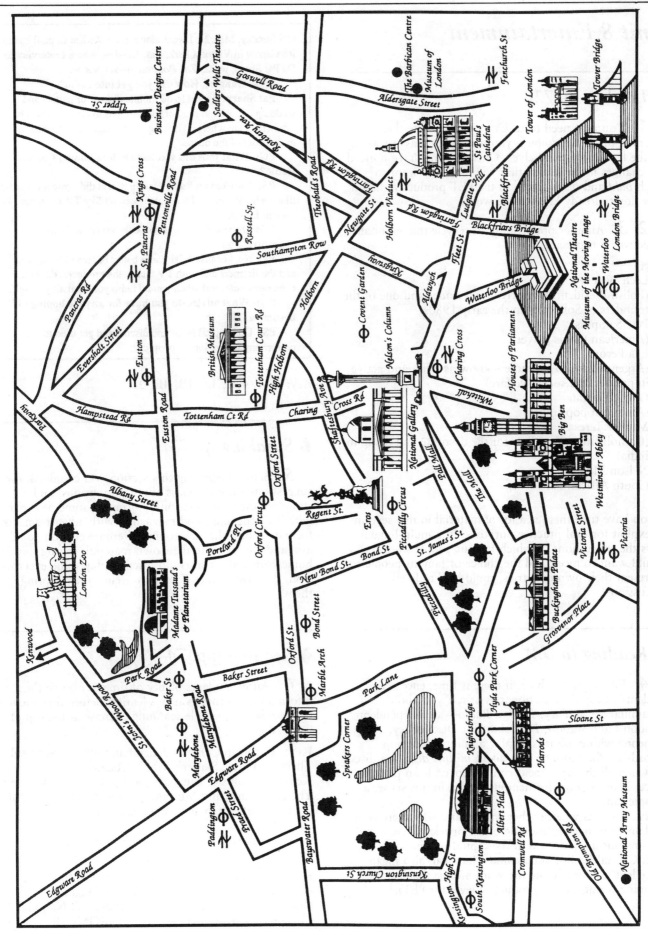

Unit 8 Entertainment

◆ Lead-in (p. 72)

1 You may need to teach or demonstrate the meaning of *upside down* if you want your class to work on the lead-in by themselves. Once students have noticed the changes in the illustration you may also want to teach *bald* and *beard* (both in the PET productive list) if they don't already know these words.

2, 3 Another opportunity to recycle the nationality adjectives if necessary!

Key:
A Lech Wałesa
   (Polish President, formerly union leader and one of the founders of Solidarity in the early 1980s)
B Pete Sampras
   (American tennis player)
C Eva Peron
   (Argentinian or Argentine – know as Evita and active in politics and social welfare)
D Gloria Estefan
   (American pop singer)
E Mother Teresa
   (Catholic nun who cares for the destitute and dying in India)
F Nelson Mandela
   (South African President)

If you have time there is a lot of material in this section to exploit for oral practice purposes. In a multi-lingual class the suggestions of which famous people students would want to meet, and the choice of famous people to represent their own countries, could lead to lively discussions!

◆ Reading (p. 73)

4 Either pre-teach or, if there is time, encourage students to use their dictionaries or ask you about unfamiliar vocabulary: *Capital Radio* – an independent London radio station; *DJ* – short for Disc Jockey, someone whose job it is to play and introduce pop records on the radio or at a disco; *mobile disco* – a disco in which all the equipment can be moved from place to place; *demo* – short for demonstration, in this sense, a sample tape.

Ask students whether they understand why there is an exclamation mark in the title of the article. There could be three meanings: a job in the capital – London; a job with Capital Radio; and *capital* which can also mean 'excellent' (although like the word *mobile* this last meaning is outside the productive level for PET).

ON Sunday, May 21, I went along to the KitKat Capital Radio Roadshow in Victoria Park, East London, where I interviewed DJ Pat Sharp, *writes Zak Poulton, from London.*

Press Ganger: How did you get into radio?

Pat Sharp: I used to do mobile discos for parties and weddings. I used to send off demo tapes to radio stations but I didn't get anywhere. Then I got a manager who helped me to the front of the queue.

PG: What jobs did you have before joining Capital Radio?

PS: I worked on Radio One first, and did some local radio like Radio Mercury. I have also been on Sky TV for some time in Europe.

PG: Do you think you will ever leave radio to concentrate on TV?

PS: No, because I like radio better because it's just you and the listeners and with TV there's the producer, director, cameraman etc. and when you do radio you do it all yourself.

PG: What advice do you have for anyone hoping to become a DJ?

PS: Do hospital radio and discos, and get used to performing before lots of people.

Key: 3, 1, 4, 2; 3A, 1B, 4D, 2C

◆ Speaking (p. 73)

5 Before beginning this section you could ask for suggestions from the class about pop groups, and stimulate their imagination by bringing some newspapers with TV schedules, and magazines with advertisements for videos into the classroom. Alternatively you could ask students to bring their own material, setting this as a homework task. You could offer to play some excerpts from their own tapes if they can remember to bring them!

◆ Reading (pp. 74–77)

6 Allow students plenty of time to absorb the information on these various leaflets before they move on to the relatively simple scanning exercise at the top of page 76.

Key: Barbican Centre - dance band music; National Theatre - plays; Sadler's Well's Theatre - dance; Kenwood - music; Business Design Centre - modern art; The National Army Museum - soldiers; The National Gallery - art; MOMI - cinema and TV.

7 Pre-teach *extract* – a small part from a longer piece of writing or music

Key: London Museum - 7; Barbican Centre - 3; National Theatre - 6; Sadler's Well's Theatre - 5; Kenwood - 4; Business Design Centre - 2; National Army Museum - 1; National Gallery - 9; MOMI - 8

◆ *Listening* (p. 78)

8 Before playing the tape you need to encourage the class to try and identify with being a visitor to London. There is a map on page 33 of this teacher's book which you can photocopy for the class to use as a preliminary exercise. If there is time try to get them to plan a short trip (two or three days) to London using the information on the map as well as the material in exercise 6. Play the tape right through without stopping between each short dialogue and then, if necessary, repeat the tape.

Key: 1 the National Theatre. **2** the Museum of London. **3** the Barbican Centre. **4** MOMI. **5** the Birmingham Royal Ballet

---

◆ *Grammar* (pp. 78–79)

9 The list in the student's book covers some of the most common phrasal verbs. However, there are others in the PET productive list which students need to know. You might like to devise a way with your class for them to remember these verbs – perhaps learning them alphabetically or drawing a vocabulary 'flower'. It would not be a good idea to try and cover all these at once; try concentrating on one at a time over a period of a few weeks, and then use the examples below to revise the meanings.

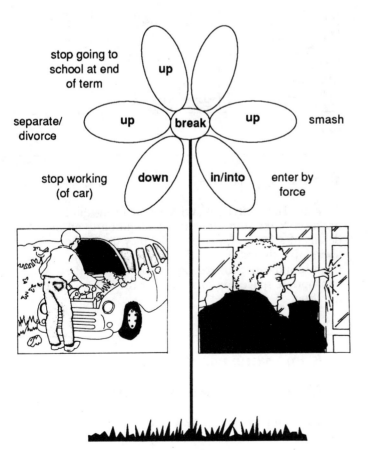

break down – My car broke down yesterday. (failed to go)
break in/into – A man broke into the art gallery and stole two valuable paintings. (entered by force)
break up – We break up for the summer holidays in June. (finish school for the holidays)
break up – My parents have broken up. (separated)
break up – Thieves broke up the furniture in the museum. (smashed into pieces)
call someone up – She called me up in the middle of the night (phoned)
call in – Why don't you call in and see me sometime? (visited)
care about – I really care about Vlasta – she's been a good friend for many years.
care for – I don't care for modern ballet. (dislike – can also be used in the positive, i.e. like)
come on – Come on or we'll miss the start of the concert! (hurry up)
hold up – I'm sorry I'm late – I was held up in a traffic jam. (delayed)
keep on – She kept on dancing until the age of seventy. (continued)
keep up – You're doing very well – keep up the good work! (continue to maintain standards, make an effort)
knock out – The fall from his bike knocked him out. (made him unconscious)
leave out – He left out a number of details in his report. (omitted)
ring back – She rang back after ten minutes (phoned)
ring up – I'll ring you up tomorrow evening. (phone)
set off – They set off/for work/on their trip at 7 a.m. (start/started)
set out – They set out on their journey quite late in the day. (started)

10 Key: **1** put up (raised) **2** look after (take care of) **3** went off (fired) **4** goes with (matches) **5** going on (happening) **6** look up (try to find) **7** take off (leave the ground) **8** Turn/Put off (switch out) **9** took down (wrote) **10** went on (continued) **11** putting through (connecting) **12** take up (start as a hobby) **13** went off (stopped working) **14** Look out (take care) **15** getting along (manage to live with) **16** gone out (stopped burning) **17** put off (postponed) **18** turned into (became) **19** take away (subtract) **20** turn on (switch on)

11 Before starting on this you could (depending on time available) try some quick oral practice. For example: 'Think of five things you want your partner to do, e.g. stand up, give me your book etc.' You could turn it into a game with students in teams, gaining (or losing!) points for understanding and carrying out the instructions. Or you could ask your class to give you these orders instead! Alternatively, try a game traditionally called 'Simon says . . .' in the UK. (Choose any name you want – it doesn't have to be 'Simon'.) One person stands in front of the class and calls out instructions, e.g. 'Simon says put your hands on your head'. Everybody has to imitate the action. However, if the caller says 'Put your hands on your head' without first saying 'Simon says' anyone who then imitates the action is out of the game.

12 **Key:** 1 close/shut 2 throw/drop 3 Queue/ Stand/Wait 4 feed 5 touch/stroke
(Students may come up with other plausible alternatives; the first answers given above are those from the original notices.)

◆ *Speaking (p. 80)*

13 This exercise revises some of the language already practised in exercise 5. The task here provides practice in the kind of pairwork/role play that students might encounter in Section IV of the Oral. The prompts practise the language for this kind of interaction, and the task should be prepared initially in conjunction with the written support. Make sure that students don't rely on the printed prompts once they start the role play. They should just focus on the TV programmes. Allow time for people to look at the television programmes and check that they understand the roles they each have to play before working with their partner. You and the class could vote on the most persuasive argument!

◆ *Speaking and Writing (p. 80)*

14 Check that students have written down correct question forms before they go on to interview four people. For example:
Which records/tapes/CDs have you chosen? or
What did you choose to take with you? or
Which book would you take with you? or
Why have you chosen that? or
Why did you choose that?

15 The oral follow-up in this exercise can be taken a stage further and set as a written task for homework in the form of a short report. Alternatively, use the Further Practice for this unit on page 131 for greater variety at this stage, but make sure that the students keep the results of their interviews. In this way you can return to the material later and use it for a written task.

◆ *Reading (p. 81)*

16 Students might like to guess whereabouts in Spain this photograph was taken. The answer is Granada.
This text is quite difficult and students will probably need to look up some of the vocabulary. If they work in small groups, however, they can pool their information to save time. The kinds of questions they write will obviously vary, but check that they are written correctly before being passed on to another group. Questions

could cover the title of the picture; who took the photograph; when it was taken; what different people are doing; what kinds of objects the writer mentions; why Ludmila Gregg likes this picture.

◆ *Reading (p. 82)*

17 This exercise builds on similar practice in Unit 7 (exercise 21) and contrasts with the reading subskills in exercise 16. You might like to divide the task so that a couple of the examples (those related to the topic – A and B) can be worked through in class with the remaining ones being done independently for homework.

18 Key: 1C 2E 3B 4D 5A

◆ *Listening (p. 83)*

19 This task also begins with further practice in reading skills (scanning for specific information) as a preparation for an intensive listening exercise.

Key: English; Wednesday July 4; John Metcalf

20 Pre-teach *stalls* and *circle*, or use exercise 22 to explain these words.
Key:

Opera	Date	Alt. Date	No of Tickets	First Choice Seat Location	Alternative Seat Location	Ticket Price	TOTAL	Box Office Use
Rosenkavalier								
Freischütz								
Così fan tutte								
Barber								
Otello								
Tornrak	4/7	–	2	FRONT STALLS	BACK STALLS	£15	£30	
						TOTAL	£30	

◆ *Speaking (p. 84)*

21 This exercise recycles earlier form-filling practice. Make sure students pay attention to all the details of a form. If, for example, they do not have an alternative choice of date (for whatever reason), remind them to indicate their response with a line in the appropriate space/box to show that they have read the question.

◆ *Know your vocabulary (p. 85)*

22 ENTRANCE or WAY IN; EXIT or WAY OUT.

23 Students should be able to pick out the title of the play, the day and the date, the time of the performance, the row and seat number and the cost of the ticket. (Note *inc VAT* – including Value Added Tax at 17.5%, but students do not need to know this. The other figures refer to the fact that this child's ticket was booked on Jan. 17th.)

24 Checklist:

1 classical	6 popular	11 opera
2 comedian	7 performance	12 ballet /'bælei/
3 musician	8 cloakroom	13 screen
4 interval	9 sculpture	14 musical
5 audience	10 antique	

25 This exercise is designed to be used as a quick written check, although it could be exploited for oral practice if you wish.

Unit 9 Work, Sports, Hobbies

◆ Lead-in (p. 86)

1 The cartoon provides an opportunity to check that students know the difference in spelling between *practice* (noun) and *practise* (verb), both of which are pronounced /'præktis/ ; (also worth reminding class about *advice* /əd'vais/ and *advise* /əd'vaiz/¹).
Students will probably need to refresh their memories about these faces, which originally appeared in Unit 1 exercise 2 (page 6).
Pre-teach *hobby* – something that you enjoy doing in your spare time.

Key: Swiss – sport; Malaysian – stamps; Spanish – soldiers; Italian – drums

◆ Listening (p. 87)

2 Make sure the students look carefully at the visuals and then ask them to predict what they can expect to hear. This is always a valuable pre-listening strategy which they can be trained to employ in the listening section of the PET.

Key: Jack C Sophie D Leo D Daniella D

3 Ideally the listening task will have sparked off some discussion of hobbies. If you think it is appropriate, tell the class about your own hobbies either present or past as a warm-up to the oral activity. Or you may know of people with unusual hobbies, and this could provide further material for discussion.

◆ Reading (pp. 88–89)

4 Pre-teach the vocabulary which falls outside PET productive level: *yacht* (pronounced /jɒt/) – a boat with sails or a motor, used for racing or pleasure trips (the visual should help!); *cork* – a soft light substance which forms the bark of a type of Mediterranean tree and floats on water; *pond* – a small area of water that is smaller than a lake; *striking* – unusual.

Key: 1 eight (years old)   2 to find out what the weather will be like   3 yes   4 no   5 classical   6 pop music

5 Pre-teach the vocabulary which falls outside PET productive level: *Dame* – in Britain, Dame is a title given to a woman as a special honour because of important service or work that she has done (Judi Dench received her honour for her services to the theatre); *set* – in this context means the furniture and scenery on stage for a play; *boarding school* – a school where pupils live during the term.

Key: 1, 3, 4, 6, 9, 10 – all ticked

◆ *Speaking* (p. 90)

6 This opening exercise should be done fairly quickly and students should be encouraged to give brief responses as to why or why not they would be interested in any of the jobs. For example: *I love cooking* or *I'm not interested in computers.*

◆ *Reading* (p. 90)

7 Pre-teach *hotshot* – a slang word for a very impressive person; *upmarket* – an adjective used to describe commercial products, services etc. that are relatively expensive and of superior quality.

Key: He's only 17 but has his own computer company – accept answers along these lines.

◆ *Speaking* (p. 91)

8 This task is obviously very open-ended and should provide plenty of opportunity for discussion.

9 You may need to brief yourself on average wages for these jobs in various countries depending on your own teaching situation.

◆ *Writing* (p. 91)

10 You should adapt these headings for an appropriate CV to suit the students' own background and in the light of what a job applicant would expect to submit. The format of such documents varies from country to country, so feel free to add to or delete these headings! The point is, however, that at the end of the course students are getting further opportunity to practise reproducing information needed to identify themselves.

◆ *Listening* (p. 92)

11 Make sure students know how to pronounce the names of these various sports before they listen to the tape.

Key: tennis, table tennis, hockey, mountain biking, swimming (any order)

Belgium	2	Italy	2
Holland	0	Greece	0
Egypt	3	Scotland	1
France	1	Wales	2

◆ *Speaking* (p. 93)

12 Make sure that you put a time limit on the speeches – maybe two minutes at the most! If you want, you can also organise a final in which all the 'survivors' from each group of four are put in one balloon. They will have to write a fresh speech, but this time it could be done as a group activity, so that in a sense the 'survivor' represents her/his group in the final. Allow a minute for each speech and vote for one outright winner. Once the written prompts have been discussed and practised in the lesson, the actual writing task could be set for homework, and the Balloon Debate held in the next lesson.

◆ *Grammar* (pp. 93–94)

13 If necessary, revise the way in which the present perfect tense is formed by highlighting a few examples in class, so that students can note the verb pattern. It may also be necessary to remind students of when this tense is used (although this is explained in the Student's Book) by drawing a diagram to show how the past and present are connected. Some students find it helpful to have a visual representation of the 'time dimension'. An example is included here, but you might want to devise your own.

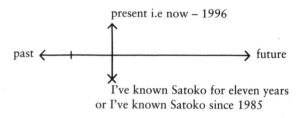

present i.e now – 1996

past ← → future

I've known Satoko for eleven years
or I've known Satoko since 1985

This particular exercise concentrates on the adverbial word order appropriate to PET level.

14 **Key:** 1 ever 2 yet 3 yet 4 never 5 just
6 already 7 never 8 just

15 This exercise practises the uses of *for* and *since* with the present perfect tense.

16 **Key:** 1 for 2 since 3 for 4 since 5 since

◆ *Reading* (p. 95)

17 As a warm-up exercise ask students to scan the four reading texts in order to answer question 1. Then ask students to read the texts carefully for detail. They will come across words they don't necessarily know (and certain words in these texts are outside the level), but they should understand that this will not prevent them from answering questions 1–8. It is very important to encourage students to realise how much can be answered without knowing the meaning of every single word. This confidence should enable them to cope with the reading section of the PET, especially Parts 3 and 4 of the Reading Paper.

Key: 1 to give people advice
2 A walking in the country
  B swimming pool rules
  C using a lake
  D walking in winter
3 D 4 for swimmers 5 B and C 6 A
7 lakes do not warm up like the sea
8 to make sure you know how deep it is

◆ *Speaking* (p. 96)

18 Ask students to look first at the pictures and then at the prompts. You can brainstorm for all kinds of reasons as to why one picture is preferable to another, but when you move on to the game make sure students are not looking at the prompts but at the pictures. Pick students at random and tell them that they are either A or B. Put the question, e.g. 'Abdul, why do you want to have this picture?' Students must respond within five seconds without repeating a reason that has already been given by someone else. The game can be played until one student is left, or you can stop it at any point depending on the time available. Alternatively, divide the class into two: A and B. 'A' students must try to persuade you to buy 'Bravo!', 'B' students ' Shot!'. The side which puts up the most persuasive (and grammatically correct) reasons wins!

◆ *Writing* (p. 96)

19 Students should begin this exercise by working in pairs to decide which of these sports they would choose. The letter is best set as a homework task, but the kind of information which needs to be included in the letter should be discussed in class. Ask students to suggest what they might want to comment on in terms of food and accommodation. Encourage them to read the instructions carefully and to cover all the points: food, accommodation, sports activities, and whether they are enjoying themselves or not. As the letter is being written during the course, make sure that they know which tense they will need to use, i.e. present continuous.

◆ *Know your vocabulary* (p. 97)

20 **Key:** kicking, throwing, jogging, doing exercises, relaxing

21 **Key:** plus, minus, times, divided by, equals, per cent

22 **Key:** inverted commas, full stop, semi-colon, brackets, exclamation mark, apostrophe, comma, colon, question mark, hyphen

23 **Key:** A(nno) D(omini) – in the year of the Lord; before noon; arrives; B(efore) C(hrist); care of; centimetre(s); continued; departs; gram(s); kilometre(s); Limited; maximum; minute or minimum; take special note of; pages; please turn over; Road; Square; Street; Christmas; year

24 **Checklist:**
1 guard   5 hydrofoil   9 duvet
2 detective 6 hovercraft 10 hijack
3 stadium   7 army
4 electronic 8 receptionist

Unit 10 Practice Test

Ideally this practice test should be used as close as possible to the date of the real test, and not immediately after students have completed Unit 9. Before the students take this replica test, you should make sure that they are familiar with the overall structure of the test (see Introduction, page 9 and the overview of the PET on page 7). You will also need to make sure you allow sufficient class time, which may mean rearranging lessons or liaising with colleagues. At the back of the students' book you will find examples of the answer sheets that students will be given in the exam. These may be used for the practice test. If you decide not to use them, go through them with your students before the exam and check they know how to fill them in.

Reading and Writing: This should be taken in one complete session lasting 1½ hours. If there is simply no way of making arrangements for this length of time to be available, then you can split the Reading and Writing allowing 45 minutes for each with students taking the Reading in one lesson and the Writing in another. However, this does not replicate the test situation or give them the desirable experience of a timed test.

Listening: Allow approximately 20–25 minutes. This need not be taken on the same day as the Reading and Writing paper, but it obviously has to be completed in one stage.

Speaking: The Speaking Test can only be taken by candidates in pairs. In order for students to gain the most benefit from the oral practice material, you should attempt to use the material with each pair in one session (without students telling each other what the material is about), allowing approximately 10–12 minutes for each pair. There is more information on how to conduct the Speaking Test on page 44, in conjunction with the prompt materials.

Key and Sample Answers

◆ Reading (p. 98)

Marking: 1 mark for each correct answer unless indicated otherwise.

Part 1: 5 marks
1. D   2. C   3. C   4. A   5. B

Part 2: 5 marks
6. C   7. F   8. A   9. E   10. G

Part 3: 10 marks
11. B   12. B   13. B   14. B   15. A   16. A   17. A
18. A   19. B   20. B

Part 4: 5 marks
21. D   22. C   23. A   24. C   25. A

Part 5: 10 marks
26. B   27. C   28. A   29. B   30. C   31. D   32. A
33. B   34. C   35. D

Total marks for Reading section:
5 + 5 + 10 + 5 + 10 = 35

Raw mark: 1 2 3 4 5 6 7 8 9 10 11 12 13 14 15 16 17 18 19

Scaled mark: 1 1 2 3 4 4 5 6 6   7   8   9   9 10 11 11 12 13 14

Raw mark: 20 21 22 23 24 25 26 27 28 29 30 31 32 33 34 35

Scaled mark: 14 15 16 16 17 18 19 19 20 21 21 22 23 24 24 25

Convert the raw mark to the scaled mark so that the final mark represents 25% of the complete test.

◆ Writing (p. 107)

Part 1: 5 marks
1 mark for each correct answer (ignore minor spelling mistakes which do not affect the structural accuracy)

1. . . . has a lot/many different (kinds of) colleges.
2. . . . teach music.
3. . . . necessary to play (at least) two instruments.
4. . . . in public is frightening/frightens/can frighten/ some students/makes some students frightened.
5. . . . prefer to teach/teaching music.

Part 2: 10 marks, 1 mark for each correct answer; see the marked student samples for guidance.

Application Form
CAMP AUSTRALIA SUMMER CAMPS

SURNAME (6) ....

FIRST NAME(S) (7) ....

HOME ADDRESS (8) .... *Must include country*

NATIONALITY (9) .... *appropriate adjective*

DATE OF BIRTH (day/month/year) (10) ....

SEX (11) .... *male/female*

How many weeks can you work?

(12) .... *any appropriate*

What sport(s) can you play?

(13) .... *any appropriate*

Why do you want to work for Camp Australia?

(14) .... *brief response*

SIGNATURE

(15) .... *NOT printed*

1 mark for each correct answer = 10 marks

Application Form
CAMP AUSTRALIA SUMMER CAMPS

SURNAME (6) *Huzac*

FIRST NAME(S) (7) *Hélène*

HOME ADDRESS (8) *Av. de la Besse, Ste. Férèole 19270 France*

NATIONALITY (9) *French*

DATE OF BIRTH (day/month/year) (10) *19/04/73*

SEX (11) *female*

How many weeks can you work?

(12) *8 weeks*

What sport(s) can you play?

(13) *basketball, volleyball*

Why do you want to work for Camp Australia?

(14) *I want to meet people of many nationalities*

SIGNATURE

(15) *Hélène Huzac*

10 marks

Part 3: 10 marks

Award up to 5 marks for completion of the task. Students should give some information about what they are doing and then specify what they find boring. Give credit to answers which convey a genuine feeling as to why certain things are boring.

Award up to 5 marks for structural accuracy, i.e. use of appropriate tenses, range of vocabulary within this level, correct informal ending.

The sample answers below give a guide to how these marking criteria are implemented (task + accuracy).

I'm spending a nice time here, although I (~~try and~~) Think There are too many activities for us, and sometimes it is very tiring for me. We're always going to and fro, after tennis. We have to go to play golf, and afterwards We have to go fishing, and so every day. ~~I~~ When I feel very tired I usually Think in The wonderful figure I'll get After that. I have met many wonderful People here, and the most I like to do is going to the disco in the night. I (~~no wish~~) wish you a nice hollidays too, and If you want, you could come here ~~with~~ with me, Please Think about it
Kises ~~Pet~~

2 + 4 = 6
neglects to mention boring aspects

I'm doing ~~this but~~ a lot of things but I'm not finding some parts of the programme rather interesting because sometime we have to go to fishing and I think that this is very bored. ~~I'm~~ I'm playing some Sports that I like it but ~~I~~ have another sports that I don't it so sometimes I'm boring. I hope

you are better than me because I'm working rather in this Camp and I thought that I came here for holidays. I'm ~~looking~~ waiting to see you.
Your friend
~~[signature]~~

3 + 3 = 6
Some confusion between 'bored' + 'boring' although task is completed reasonably well.

We are living in nice little bungalous beside a lake. I like this very much because there are alot of opportunities to do sports. We can go swimming, fishing and sailing. And now listen very well: I'm attending a surfing-course!! First I thought, this is nothing for me, but now I like it very much. I'm already quite good - if there's not too much wind! There are also some parts of our programme I don't like. Every evening we have to go to a hotel in the next village ~~for~~ our dancing-course! It's always very boring because the music is very old-fashioned. Also the bicycle-tours are really stupid! We can't rest when we want, we have always to be in an exactly line.
Well, I hope you're enjoying your holidays in England and you're having a great time with your friends.
With love, Katharinna

5 + 5 = 10 A very good answer despite length.

Total marks for Writing section: 5 + 10 + 10 = 25
The raw score represents the correct percentage and
therefore no additional calculation need be made.

For the total mark for the Paper, add the converted
reading score and the raw writing score together.

◆ *Listening (p.110)*

Play the tape straight through without stopping it
between questions. The timing of pauses and checking
times are the same as in the real examination. Candidates
are allowed 12 minutes at the end of the Listening Test to
transfer their answers to the answer sheet.

Part 1: 7 marks
1. D   2. C   3. B   4. C   5. A   6. B   7. D

Part 2: 6 marks
8. C   9. D   10. B   11. C   12. C   13. A

Part 3: 6 marks, 1 mark for each correct answer; see the
marked student samples for guidance.

Part 4: 6 marks
20. A   21. A   22. B   23. B   24. A   25. B

Total marks for the Listening section:
7 + 6 + 6 + 6 = 25

Public Meeting : SAVE OUR HOSPITAL

* (14) _money_ is what we need most!

  for : advertising

      printing posters

  (15) _T-shirts_ and badges

* suggestions : organise a (16) _disco_

                  or a (17) _concert_

* can have the school hall without paying!

* 3 months from now : (18) _food festival_

  necessary to contact papers, radio

  and TV

* Committee want suggestions over

  (19) _famous people/person to invite_
  1 mark for each correct
  answer = 6 marks

Public Meeting : SAVE OUR HOSPITAL

* (14) _Comite_ is what we need most!   (0)

  for : advertising

      printing posters

  (15) _t-shirt_ and badges   (1)

* suggestions : organise a (16) _disco_   (1)

                  or a (17) _musician
                  concert_   (1)

* can have the school hall without paying!

* 3 months from now : (18) _food festival_
                                (1)

  necessary to contact papers, radio

  and TV

* Committee want suggestions over

  (19) _famous people can be invited_   (1)
       5 marks

Public Meeting : SAVE OUR HOSPITAL

* (14) _money_ is what we need most!   (1)

  for : advertising

      printing posters

  (15) _tee shirts_ and badges   (1)

* suggestions : organise a (16) _disco_ (1)

                  or a (17) _concert_
                                (1)

* can have the school hall without paying!

* 3 months from now : (18) _food festival_
                                (1)

  necessary to contact papers, radio

  and TV

* Committee want suggestions over

  (19) _the famous person invite_   (1)
       6 marks

◆ *Speaking*

The various sections of the Speaking Test should be conducted without obvious breaks between the four sections. Sometimes Sections 3 and 4 may be linked, in that the topic in Section 3 may be further developed in Section 4, but not necessarily so.

Allow approximately 3 minutes for each section of the test. Prompt material for the Speaking Test can be found in the colour section in the middle of this Teacher's Book. This should be taken out and cut down the middle to provide the prompts for Student A and Student B.

Section 1: In this section, after the initial greetings candidates will be asked to find out some basic information about each other. If they know each other the examiner will ask them to pretend that they don't. They need to practise asking questions which elicit personal details: where they live, what they do, why they are learning English, their families etc. It is valuable practice, to go through the mechanics of the Speaking part of the test so that students know what to expect in the real test situation.

The questions should be simple and straightforward, e.g. What's your name? How do you spell that? Where do you live? Why are you learning English?

Section 2: In this section students will receive some prompt material and can expect to develop a short conversation. This will be based on a situation which the examiner will describe, in which students may have to give directions, discuss their needs, reply to requests etc. in a role play situation. Encourage your students to ask for clarification or repetition if they haven't understood something the first time.

Show the students the picture prompts. Tell them that they are going to organise a shopping trip for themselves to a city which they have not visited before. Ask them to plan how they will travel, what they will do when they get there and any other preparations they will have to make. Allow them a few seconds to think about it and then ask them whether they have understood or whether they would like you to repeat it. Then ask one of the students to start the conversation and allow them 2–3 minutes to work through the task before you intervene to end what they are saying. Use an appropriate expression like 'Well, I hope you have a good day' to bring things to a natural conclusion.

Section 3: In this section the speaking task is slightly different once again in that students have to describe where people are and what they are doing. Tell Student A to turn the picture prompt over and look at the photograph on the other side. Student B should also be able to see the photograph. Ask Student A to talk about the photograph for approximately 1 minute. Then ask Student B to turn their picture prompt over and do the same.

For your information: in Student B's photograph the girl is ten years old and she is jumping in a fountain in Luxembourg. Student A's photograph shows the same girl, but three years older, stroking a horse in Bruges, Belgium.

Students are not expected to know the word 'stroke'; you can supply it if you think it would be helpful but otherwise accept descriptions like 'She is playing with/talking to/touching' etc. At an appropriate point allow them a few seconds to look at each other's photos before moving on to the last section.

Section 4: In the PET, Sections 3 and 4 are loosely linked. Continue the conversation along the lines established in the previous section, but this time encourage your students to talk about whether as young children they enjoyed doing what the girl is doing. Why did they enjoy it? Were they allowed to do it? Why do most children love jumping in puddles or playing in water? Did they enjoy playing with animals? Perhaps they were afraid to touch animals. What sort of things did they do as children? Try to encourage them to express their likes and dislikes, their experiences and habits. You should allow about 5 minutes for Sections 3 and 4 together.

Marking: Draw up a simple grid on which you can broadly assess each student on the following four criteria:

- the ability to use accurate and appropriate grammatical structures and vocabulary
- the ability to express what one wants to say fluently and coherently
- the ability to pronounce what one says intelligibly
- the ability to complete each task by participating in appropriate interactive strategies

The assessor will award up to a maximum of 5 marks for each of the four criteria, but from March 1997 the interlocutor has also been required to award a global mark for each candidate at the end of the test. The global mark is an impression mark based on a single scale from 0 - 5 and is awarded independently of the detailed marks. In this way a candidate receives assessments from both examiners. In order to reach the standard required for a minimum overall pass at PET a candidate needs a score of 3 on the global scale.

It is up to you to decide what use you make of any marking procedures. The guidelines described here can give you an idea of how your students would fare in a real test, but you should not employ the suggested mark scheme to give any kind of definitive result. One of the most useful ways to exploit the practice test would be to use the 'results' of each component part of the test to indicate students' strengths and weaknesses and which areas they need to work on in order to be fully prepared for all sections of the test.

Further Practice

No marks are allocated to these exercises as they are intended for practice purposes and not assessment. However, it is entirely up to you if you want to give your students marks. If you do, it would be a good idea to look first at how the practice test is marked (pages 40–44).

Unit 1

◆ *Writing (form-filling) (p.116)*

Example:

◆ *Grammar (reported speech) (p. 117)*

Key: 1 . . . Maria how old she was/old Maria was.
2 . . . (Maria) what she/Maria did in her free time.
3 . . . Juan when he arrived/had arrived in England/when Juan had arrived in England.
4 . . . (that) she missed her family.
5 . . . she wanted to be an interpreter when she grew up.
6 . . . Juan whether he wanted to be an interpreter too/ whether Juan wanted to be an interpreter too when he grew up.

Woodford College

Surname/Family name: ....SZLOTARSKI.............................

Other names: ...MIRKA JOLANTA.................. Sex:...Female...

Address: ...Ul. Janowskiego 47..........................
...........WARSAW 03-526 POLAND...............

Nationality: ....Polish..................... Date of Birth:..26/6 74...

Occupation: ....Student..

Have you any brothers or sisters? ...No...........................

How did you hear about the college? ...My friend studied at the college for two years and she told me about it....................

Do you want us to arrange accommodation for you? (please tick)

Yes ☑
No ☐

Do you smoke? Yes ☐
No ☑

Have you any special requests? eg. food, religion ...I would like to be with a family which has children. Also I do not eat meat...

Signature ....Mazolei.............. Date ...22/11/90...

◆ *Writing (a note) (p. 117)*

Example:

Kamal,

How are you? I am fine.

Would you like to meet me in London one day? I am usually free at the weekend. How about Saturday June 7ᵗʰ or Sunday June 8ᵗʰ? I can catch the 08.15 train and meet you at the station.

Ring me soon!

John

Unit 2

◆ *Reading (notices and signs) (p. 118)*

Pre-teach *prohibit* or allow students to guess.

Key: 1 7   2 in the street   3 4, 5, 9   4 in a park
5 on a bus   6 10, 11   7 2, 3
8 you must keep quiet/you must not make a noise
9 1, 8   10 d

◆ *Writing (a letter) (p. 119)*

Example:

Dear Ruth

---------- There is a small space at the front of the house, but still enough size to park a car and also garage at the back of the house. The house is quite old and also it is quite big. It has got really nice front door too. I share the house with several people and my room is on the first floor. The size of the room is quite small but I've got a comfortable bed, a desk with a lamp and a lovely chest of drawers, also a gas ring and wash basin so I can cook something in my room which is very useful.
    There is a bus stop about 5 minutes on foot and I can go to town by that bus.
Write to me soon, Love
                        Ami

Unit 3

◆ *Reading (gapped text) (p. 120)*

If students find the example confusing, you may want to highlight the difference between *lend* and *borrow*:
lend – if you lend someone money or something that you own, you allow them to have it or use it for a period of time; *borrow* – if you borrow something that belongs to someone else, they allow you to have it or use it for a period of time.

Key: 1 B   2 A   3 C   4 D   5 B   6 A   7 C   8 D   9 A
10 C

◆ *Speaking (role-play) (p. 121)*

Before asking students to do this exercise, you might like to pre-teach the suggested prompts in another context (e.g. buying furniture) so that you can direct the pairs to focus on the role-play from the moment they read their role cards.

    Allow time for the class to listen to at least a few pairs of students acting out their role-play, even if you can't allow time for everyone.

Unit 4

◆ *Listening (visual multiple choice) (p. 122)*

If you think your students don't know the word *sour* and you don't want them to guess it, then preteach – something tastes sour if it has a sharp taste like a lemon for example; sour milk tastes unpleasant because it is no longer fresh. (NB *bitter* – can also be used to describe sharp, unpleasant tastes such as orange peel or coffee dregs.)

Key: 1 A   2 C   3 A   4 C   5 B

◆ *Writing ('free' but within a framework) (p. 123)*

Example:

I would like to cook a meal for my teacher Ms. Lingford because she does not know very much about Thai food. She came to Thailand six months and she is very interested in cooking. At weekends she sometimes comes to my house and watches my mother cooking different Thai foods. My menu would include:

    Sour Prawn Soup (not too many chillies!)

    Chicken in Peanut and Coconut Sauce

    Beef and Water Chestnuts

    Thai rice

Kumaree's Thai Burger
I would put some raw shrimps mixed with soya sauce and lemon grass. Then I would cook some onions with ginger and put it all inside a warm bun. It would taste very delicious!

Unit 5

◆ *Reading (notices) (p. 124)*
Key: 1 D 2 B 3 B 4 B 5 D

◆ *Reading (for detail) (p. 125)*
Key: 1 F 2 T 3 T 4 T 5 T 6 F 7 F 8 F

Unit 6

◆ *Reading and Writing (a letter) (p. 126)*
Example:

Dear Sir/Madam,
I would like to book two single rooms at The State House for four nights from September 2nd to September 5th. If possible I would like rooms with a shower. Thank you.
Yours faithfully,

◆ *Reading (a gapped text) (p. 127)*
Key: 1 A 2 B 3 D 4 C 5 B 6 A 7 B 8 A 9 C 10 C

Unit 7

◆ *Reading (for detail and general meaning) (pp. 128–129)*
Key: 1 A 2 C 3 D 4 B 5 C

♦ *Speaking (describing people, places, activities) (p. 129)*

Key: The photograph shows:
a girl sitting on a bench outside/in front of a school/
sports centre
perhaps she's waiting for someone
she's talking to another girl on a bicycle
a group of children are going into the building
some of the children are carrying bags

Unit 8

♦ *Listening (for specific information) (p. 130)*

Make sure students have read the questions before you
play the tape.

Key: 1 C   2 B   3 D   4 A   5 B   6 C

Unit 9

♦ *Listening (for general meaning as well as detail) (p. 132)*

Make sure the students have read the questions before
you play the tape.

Key: 1 Yes   2 Yes   3 Yes   4 No   5 No   6 No

♦ *Writing (grammar) (p. 132)*

Key: 1 . . . people write letters to penfriends/have
        penfriends.
2 . . . develop between some penfriends.
3 . . . exchange presents and photographs.
4 . . . on for years.
5 . . . can (sometimes) be disappointing (sometimes) for
    people when they meet.

Tapescripts

Notes on recordings

1 The recordings are arranged on the two cassettes as follows:

Cassette 1	Side 1	Units 1–4 (*pp. 7–36*)
	Side 2	Further Practice, Unit 4 (*p. 122*)
		Units 5–6 (*pp. 45–58*)
Cassette 2	Side 1	Units 7–8 (*pp. 67–83*)
		Further Practice, Unit 8 (*p. 130*)
		Unit 9 (*pp. 87–92*)
		Further Practice, Unit 9 (*p. 132*)
		Further Practice, Units 4, 8 and 9 (*pp. 122, 130, 132*)
	Side 2	Unit 10, Practice Test (*pp. 110–115*)

The Further Practice recordings can be heard either at the end of their respective units, or at the end of Cassette 2, Side 1. The Practice Test (Unit 10) recordings are all on Cassette 2, Side 2. Note that this is not the order followed in the coursebook, but this arrangement should prove convenient in practice.

2 For Units 1–9 and the Further Practice exercises, short recordings are repeated on the tape. Longer recordings are not repeated, and the teacher will need to rewind the tape for a second listening. The tapescripts indicate where repetitions are given: [REPEAT].

3 The Practice Test (Unit 10) includes all instructions, repetitions and pauses as in the PET examination. There should be no need to stop the tape.

Unit 1, Exercise 3 (p. 7)

ANGELA MURRAY: Um – Hello everyone – Good morning – and welcome. Some of you will already know me. My name is Angela Murray and I'm your tutor for the term. Now, before I give out your timetables, I need to complete the register for those of you who are new this term. Right. Let's begin with the row at the back of the room –

PACO GONZALEZ: Er – Paco Gonzalez.

AM: Paco – can you spell your surname for me please Paco?

PG: G-O-N-Z-A-L-E-Z.

AM: Fine. And you're Spanish?

PG: Si. I mean yes!

AM: And can you give me your date of birth?

PG: Eh?

AM: The date when you were born.

PG: Oh yes. November the twenty-ninth nineteen seventy-two.

AM: And your address?

PG: Here in England or in Spain?

AM: In England.

PG: Fifteen Pentland Gardens.

AM: Erm – Do you have a phone number?

PG: Yes. Double eight four three one.

AM: Great. Thanks Paco. Er next –

ROSA ANTONELLI: Rosa Antonelli.

AM: Rosa – oh, is that double L in Antonelli? You come from Italy?

RA: Yes. And my date of birth is April the eleventh nineteen seventy-three.

AM: Good. And your address?

RA: Two five nine Sadler Street but I can't remember my phone number.

AM: Never mind. Tell me tomorrow. Can you spell Sadler for me please.

RA: S-A-D-L-E-R Street.

AM: Right. Now I recognise the next person from last term. It's Björn isn't it and . . . [FADE]

Unit 1, Exercise 14 (p. 11)

DRIVER: Excuse me, is the Grosvenor House Hotel near here, please?

PEDESTRIAN: Um – you're not too far, um, carry on along this road –

D: Which is?

P: Sheaf Street – you're on the A sixty-seven – and when you get to the fork in the road about five minutes' driving time from here, take the right-hand fork into Brown Street and then turn first right into Furnival Street.

D: Fern Street?

P: No, Furnival – you can't miss it. Go straight down and you come to a main road. I think there's a roundabout – anyway go straight across and you're in Furnival Gate. The Grosvenor is on your right in Charter Square.

D: Great – thanks, so it's right all the way.

Unit 2, Exercise 16 (p. 18)

ESTATE AGENT: Take a seat Mr Stopes. I'll just get one of our application forms.

MR STOPES: Right.

EA: Now – you're looking for a house or a flat?

MR S: I'd like a house – if I can afford it that is.

EA: Well, I'll take down your particulars, and then I'll show you what we've got available. . . Um – that's Stopes. . . and have you got a daytime phone number?

MR S: There's my work number, that's two four seven six one three.

EA: Right. Now, do you want to rent or are you hoping to buy?

MR S: Oh buy – definitely buy, otherwise it's just a waste of money.

EA: Mhm. And what's your upper limit?

MR S: Pardon?

EA: How much can you afford? What is the top price you can afford to pay?

MR S: About seventy-five thousand.

EA: Seventy-five thousand. Well, that should just about get you a small house.

MR S: Great.

EA: Um, how many rooms do you want?

MR S: Um, well at least two bedrooms, lounge, kitchen, bathroom – I should say five altogether.

EA: Five – okay – and do you want central heating?

MR S: Yes! It doesn't matter whether it's gas or electric or whatever.

EA: Right. And what about the position. Do you want to be close to the city centre, outside the city?

MR S: Well I haven't got a car so I need to be fairly central, close to the station and on a bus route.

EA: So that's city centre . . . now if you wait a moment I'll check through our computer file and see what we've got . . . [FADE]

. . . .

EA: Hello, it's Miss Jones isn't it?

MISS JONES: Yes, I called in yesterday but er you were very busy and I couldn't wait.

EA: I'm sorry about that. Anyway take a seat and I'll fill in one of our forms. Now, what can we do to help you?

MISS J: I'm looking for an apartment. I'm coming to work here in about three months and so I need to start looking now.

EA: Right you are. We've a lot of flats available at the moment so it shouldn't be too difficult.

MISS J: Oh good.

EA: Have you got a daytime phone number?

MISS J: No, I'm afraid not. I travel around quite a lot so I'll have to phone you.

EA: Okay. No problem. Um, are you renting or buying?

MISS J: I want to rent to begin with, but er, if I like the job I'll probably find somewhere to buy.

EA: Mhm. And what figure have you got in mind?

MISS J: Well, not more than a hundred and twenty

pounds a week.

EA: Right. And how many rooms do you need?

MISS J: Well there's just me, so one bedroom, kitchen, sitting room and – oh – and a bathroom with a shower. And it must have a garage or a parking space.

EA: Any particular position? Erm, flats with garages in the city centre aren't easy to find.

MISS J: Well, as I've got a car I don't mind living outside the centre – not in the country mind you – and nowhere too noisy.

EA: Okay. And one more thing. Do you want a furnished or unfurnished place?

MISS J: Oh it must be furnished. I haven't any furniture of my own, not even a chair!

EA: Right. There's a flat just come onto the market which I think will interest you. I'll just get the details. . . [FADE]

Unit 2, Exercise 24 (p. 22)

1

SON: Look father, how about this bungalow? I like the garden.

FATHER: Yes, but there's no garage and nowhere to park my car unless I leave it on the road.

Listen again. [REPEAT]

2

MOTHER: Look at your bedroom Susan, it's really untidy.

SUSAN: I like it and it was Tim who left those books all over the floor, not me.

Listen again. [REPEAT]

3

GIRL: Let's see that photo – is that your family?

BOY: Yes, that's my mother and father, and my two sisters, and that's my grandad behind.

Listen again. [REPEAT]

4

MAN: I think we should look at this house first. According to the details from the estate agent it's got four rooms downstairs and three up.

WOMAN: Okay – it certainly looks as if it's got the most space.

Listen again. [REPEAT]

5

BOY: Is this where your parents live? It looks very grand.

GIRL: Oh they don't own the whole house, only the first two floors, the other two are flats.

Listen again. [REPEAT]

Unit 3, Exercise 2 (p. 24)

RADIO PRESENTER: [MUSIC – FADE UP] . . . but the value of the pound fell slightly during the day. And now to end our report here is Vivienne Smith with the tourist exchange rates for the pound. Different rates apply to travellers' cheques and you need to ask for these rates at the point of exchange.

NEWSREADER: Hello. Good news for most of you tonight as all the rates are up on yesterday's figures. As always we begin with the Australian dollar: the Bank buys at two point three three, and sells at two point one four. The Austrian schilling: sixteen fifty nine and fifteen twenty-one. The Belgian franc – the Bank buys at forty-eight seventy-two, and sells at forty-four seventy-seven. For those of you with Canadian dollars the Bank buys at two point three eight and sells at two point two one. The Finnish mark: the Bank buys at seven point six two, and sells at six point nine one. And the French franc – the Bank is buying at eight twenty-eight and selling at seven sixty-three. For the German mark the Bank buys at two point three six and sells at two point one seven. The Greek drachma: the Bank buys at three hundred and eighty-three and is selling at three hundred and fifty-eight. Onto the Dutch guilder and here. . . [FADE]

Unit 3, Exercise 8 (p. 26)

1

CLERK: Good morning. Can I help you?

CUSTOMER: Yes please. I want to send a letter to Spain. How much does it cost?

Listen again. [REPEAT]

2

CUSTOMER: I'd like to make an appointment to have my hair cut please.

RECEPTIONIST: Can you come in at two this afternoon?

Listen again. [REPEAT]

3

MAN: Can you help me please. My passport has been stolen.

POLICEMAN: Give me the details and we'll see what we can do.

Listen again. [REPEAT]

4

WOMAN: I'd like to change these travellers' cheques.

BANK CLERK: Right. You need to sign each one please.

Listen again. [REPEAT]

5

GIRL: I'd like to have this jacket cleaned – how long will it take?

SHOP ASSISTANT: Er – we have a twenty-four hour service – so this time tomorrow if you leave it now.

Listen again. [REPEAT]

Unit 3, Exercise 9 (p. 27)

1

SHOP ASSISTANT: Can I help you?
CUSTOMER: There's a sweater in the window. Do you have a larger one in my size?
SA: Um – you mean the dark one with red, blue and black squares.
C: Yes. It costs twenty-five ninety-nine.
SA: No, I'm afraid that's the only size we have.
Listen again. [REPEAT]

2

CUSTOMER: Excuse me. I want to buy a camera.
SHOP ASSISTANT: What sort of price do you want to pay?
C: Um, not too expensive – about thirty pounds.
Listen again. [REPEAT]

3

SHOP ASSISTANT: Are you being served?
CUSTOMER: No. I want to buy a box of pencils.
SA: Certainly. We have quite a choice.
C: Can you show me please?
SA: How about this one? It costs three pounds fifty.
Listen again. [REPEAT]

4

CUSTOMER: Do you sell leather jackets?
SHOP ASSISTANT: Yes. What colour did you want?
C: I'm looking for a dark green one.
SA: Yes. I think we can help you.
C: What sort of price are they?
SA: Um, a hundred and fifty pounds.
Listen again. [REPEAT]

5

CUSTOMER: Do you sell cheap tin openers?
SHOP ASSISTANT: Yes sir. The ones on the shelf behind you are only seventy-two pence.
C: Oh great.
Listen again. [REPEAT]

Unit 3, Exercise 18 (p. 30)

TOURIST GUIDE: . . . Is that everyone? All here? I've asked the coach driver to return in a couple of hours so that should give you plenty of time for shopping. Now, in a moment I'll give you all a plan of this shopping precinct. As you can see it's a new development but has been carefully designed to fit into the existing surroundings. It's built on three levels and it's quite easy to get lost (which is why it's a good idea to keep these maps with you). Now on this floor you'll find all kinds of shops from small fashion boutiques to larger department stores. For those of you interested in shoes you'll find up to eight different shoe shops, ranging from the cheap to the very expensive! If you're after presents and souvenirs however, you'll find these on the floor above. The whole area is occupied by all kinds of shops selling everything from homemade chocolate to dried flowers. For those of you living overseas, you may be interested in the special postal service, which is situated in the centre near the lifts. Anything you buy can be gift-wrapped and sent anywhere in the world! There's no extra charge for the wrapping service – you just pay the normal postal charges. Alternatively if you're buying a lot of things for yourself and you don't want to carry all the parcels with you, have them sent direct to your home address. Now on the top floor you'll find a rest area along with bars, cafes and restaurants. Well worth a visit, if only to see the roof-top gardens – drinks are also served outside so take the opportunity to have another view of the city from . . . [FADE]

Unit 4, Exercise 4 (p. 33)

GIRL: It's only me Mrs King.

MRS KING: Come on in dear!

G: I've done your shopping.

MRS K: Ah – there's a good girl – would you like a cup of tea?

G: Well that would be nice but I can't stay long, Mum wants me to collect a book for her from the library. I'll just unpack your shopping – oh – and here's your change.

MRS K: Um – will you just go through the bill for me dear so I know what I've spent – my eyes are so bad these days I can't see those tiny figures, even with my glasses on.

G: Right you are. There's your honey.

MRS K: How much was that then?

G: Er – seventy-two pence.

MRS K: That's a lot – it's gone up again.

G: Well nothing comes down these days! Um, milk – twenty-six, cornflakes – eighty-two p, er, brown bread – fifty-three, tea bags – one pound nineteen, potatoes – sixty-eight.

MRS K: Erm. Did you remember the coffee?

G: Yes, that was ninety-nine.

MRS K: Oh – ooh that's a bit cheaper than usual.

G: Er, bananas – they were fifty-six a pound, and you wanted large ones – that came to seventy-eight pence, and one tomato – seventeen.

MRS K: Seventeen!

G: Carrots – thirty-five, half a cucumber – thirty-eight, and the cauliflower – seventy-nine. There, that's the lot but if . . . [FADE]

Unit 4, Exercise 10 (p. 36)

A

BOY: I'm not very hungry, are you Suzie?

SUZIE: No – a sandwich'll do me, and we haven't much time anyway.

B: Okay – let's try that place in Queen's Square where they do sandwiches and all kinds of quick snacks – they've got a few chairs and tables outside so maybe we can get a seat.

Listen again. [REPEAT]

B

MAN: . . . so if you get there before me, go straight in and I'll join you as soon as I can. I've booked a table for eight-thirty, and the head waiter knows I might be late.

Listen again. [REPEAT]

C

MAN: Hi! Where shall we eat?

WOMAN: I thought we'd go to Chutneys.

M: Oh great. I really like being able to help myself.

W: You mean you like being able to get as much as you can on your plate.

M: For as little as possible – yes!

Listen again. [REPEAT]

D

GIRL 1:   Gosh I'm tired. Shall we have a coffee?

GIRL 2:   Oh good idea. There's a café on the top floor so we needn't leave the store.

Listen again. [REPEAT]

E

GIRL: Are you thirsty?

BOY: So-so.

G: Well we're not far from Joe's. Come on, I'll buy you a drink.

B: Oh right. Thanks!

Listen again. [REPEAT]

Further Practice, Unit 4 (p. 122)

1 What will you find in the High Street?

GIRL: Excuse me, is there a take-away restaurant in this town?

MAN: Um – there's a fish and chip shop at the bottom of the High Street, but I don't think it opens until the evening.

G: Mm, thank you.

Listen again. [REPEAT]

2 What do they order?

WAITRESS: Are you ready to order sir?

MAN: Yes please. I'll have a hot chocolate.

GIRL: And I'll have a lemon tea and chocolate cake.

Listen again. [REPEAT]

3 What has the customer brought back?

SHOP ASSISTANT: Can I help you?

WOMAN: Yes. I did some shopping here earlier today, um – fruit and vegetables and –

SA: Yes I remember.

W: Well I don't think the milk was fresh – when I tasted it it had gone sour, so perhaps you could change it.

Listen again. [REPEAT]

4 What is the complaint about?

WOMAN: Excuse me.

WAITRESS: Yes?

WOMAN: This cup is dirty, and so is the teaspoon.

WAITRESS: I'm sorry madam, I'll fetch you a clean cup.

Listen again. [REPEAT]

5 What does the man buy?

MAN: Have you got any fresh peas?

SHOP ASSISTANT: I'm afraid we're sold out, but we've plenty of frozen ones.

M: Okay, I'll have a bag of those please.

Listen again. [REPEAT]

Unit 5, Exercise 10 *(p. 45)*

DOCTOR: Come in. – Hello, come along in, it's um, let's see it's Mrs –

PATIENT: Jones doctor, you saw my little boy last week.

D: Oh yes. He's better is he?

P: Oh yes thank you.

D: So, what can I do for you?

P: It's my leg – I burnt it earlier this morning.

D: How did you do that? Just let me take off the bandage – oh dear me that is nasty.

P: Well I was standing in the kitchen, cooking, and in comes my little boy, and I bent down to pick him up and as I did so I knocked the frying pan off the stove.

D: And what were you cooking?

P: Well there was nothing in the pan except this very hot oil.

D: And it splashed over your legs?

P: Just my right leg. I put a bandage on it.

D: Um. It would have been better to leave it but never mind. Now, if you take this note to the nurse in the treatment room she'll look after you.

Unit 5, Exercise 11 *(p. 45)*

RADIO PRESENTER: [MUSIC] Welcome to this week's 'Lifestyles', the programme where we invite various people to discuss their own personal lifestyles. And in the studio today I have with me Maggie Brown and Rik Macey. Now, Maggie, you've been living in West Africa for the past year, haven't you, and you've just come back for a month's holiday.

MAGGIE BROWN: That's right – I've been teaching in a secondary school.

RP: And Rik?

RIK MACEY: Well, I'm a nurse in a large teaching hospital in the north of England.

RP: From the north of England to West Africa. Thousands of miles apart. I imagine you both lead very different lifestyles.

MB: Certainly. Compared with life in the UK my life in Dunkwa – that's the village where I live – is extremely simple. I also have a fairly long working day. I get up around six every morning (some people get up earlier for prayers), and start work at six-thirty. But then I finish around lunchtime – that's about one-thirty – and spend about two to three hours resting, if not sleeping.

RP: And everyone does that?

MB: Yes mostly. It's also the hottest part of the day, so it's better to stay indoors. And then around five every afternoon I might go shopping in the local market just to buy basic things like bread, rice, fruit, vegetables or whatever.

RP: And in the evening?

MB: Well I might stay in and work or – because I live on a compound with all the other teachers – I might drop in and have a chat – usually about work! – or someone might call on me. There's no real place to go in the sense of a restaurant or theatre, although there is a bar in the village.

RP: What about weekends?

MH: Well, then a group of us might go to the beach for a swim, or we might drive to a town in order to do some shopping. Nothing very exciting I suppose, but I actually enjoy it much more than the kind of life I used to lead when I lived in London.

RP: Mm. And Rik – very different from the kind of life you lead.

RM: Yes. I certainly don't find life simple! In fact no two days are the same. And I work shifts. That means one day I might start work at seven in the morning and finish at four in the afternoon, and another time I might start at ten in the evening and work through the night until six in the morning.

RP: And then you go home and sleep?

RM: Well, I live in one of the nurses' homes, so I don't have to go very far. And I have all my meals in the staff canteen, so I do very little shopping.

RP: And what kind of social life do you have?

RM: That's a difficult one! And my girlfriend's a policewoman, so she works shifts as well!

RP: Do you ever get to see each other?!

RM: Sometimes, yes. Sometimes we both get a weekend free together, but not often. It's difficult. And then when I do get a free weekend I'm so tired that all I want to do is sleep!

RP: But from what we said . . . [FADE]

Unit 5, Exercise 15 *(p. 47)*

1

RECEPTIONIST: Good morning, Dr Vaisey's surgery. Can I help you?

PATIENT: Yes please. I'd like to make an appointment for today if possible.

R: I'm afraid Dr Vaisey is fully booked up today. How about first thing tomorrow morning? Thursday the seventh?

P: Mm – oh all right.

R: That's tomorrow morning at eight thirty. And your name please?

P: Pryor, Ann Pryor.

R: Right. Thank you.

Listen again. [REPEAT]

2

PHARMACIST: Mr Abrahams?

MR ABRAHAMS: That's me miss.

P: Right. This is your prescription Mr Abrahams.

Take two tablets, three times a day, before meals.

MR A: I thought the doc said after meals?

P: No – these must be taken before.

MR A: Right you are. Thanks very much then.

Listen again. [REPEAT]

3

RECEPTIONIST: Yes. Name please?

MOTHER: Ingle, but it's the baby I've come about.

R: And her name?

M: Melanie – can I see a doctor, please.

R: All in good time. Melanie Ingle – address?

M: Mendip Cottage, Helfield Road, Bridgwater.

R: Bridgwater – right. What's the problem?

M: Well I left this bottle of medicine on the kitchen table, and while my back was turned I'm afraid my little girl drank it.

R: Have you brought the bottle with you?

M: Yes, yes, I've got it here.

R: Well take a seat and I'll get someone to see you straight away.

Listen again. [REPEAT]

4

DOCTOR: . . .and where does it hurt?

PATIENT: Here. . . right here. . .and it's worse when I lie down.

D: Mhm. So right across your stomach?

P: Yes, and sometimes it's so bad it goes right through to my back.

D: Lie down on the couch, and I'll see if I can feel anything. . . [FADE]

Listen again. [REPEAT]

Unit 6, Exercise 4 (p. 52)

AMY: . . . just let me spread the map out on this table, and then we'll start. Have you got paper and pencil?

TED: Yes.

A: Okay. So, where are we going to start from? Your place or mine?

T: Well as we're taking your car, could you drive over to Bristol and pick me up? Or if you'd rather not do that I'll get the bus to Bath and we'll start from there.

A: I don't mind. I'll come and collect you.

T: Great. Thanks.

A: And I'll be there by seven so we can leave early.

T: Okay. So how far shall we drive on the first day? Where shall we stop overnight?

A: Um, how about going to Stratford? There are lots of lovely villages on the way, and if it's fine we could stay a couple of nights near Stratford – it'd be cheaper than actually staying in the town itself.

T: That's a good idea. Do you want me to work out the mileage now or shall I do all that at the end and then work out the petrol costs?

A: No – let's leave that until we've decided the route.

T: Right. Do you want to go to Birmingham?

A: No I don't think so. Do you?

T: Not really. Let's keep to the countryside if we can, although I'd like to go to York because that's meant to be a very attractive city.

A: Yes, okay – but that's much further north. Where to after Stratford?

T: Well I know it's a long way but I'd really like to get to the Lake District.

A: That's miles away!

T: I know but I've never been there, and neither have you, and as we've got the time I'd like to spend a few days there, maybe based in one part, and then walk in the mountains.

A: Okay – why not. Let's spend three or four days there, and then we could drive across to York.

T: Mm. You don't want to go to Edinburgh?

A: Well I do, but it's an awful long way, and I think I'd rather go by train on another holiday. Otherwise we're going to spend all our time in the car.

T: All right. Let's spend a few days in York and drive out into the Yorkshire countryside – some of it's very wild and beautiful.

A: Right. And then?

T: Well, somewhere completely different – mm – Cambridge? – flat.

A: And boring.

T: Not at all. You can walk along the river Cam for miles – it's gorgeous.

A: Or we could take a boat.

T: Yes – whatever. But let's look around the city as well – it's years since I've been there.

A: I bet it's expensive to stay there.

T: Well we could try bed and breakfast instead of a hotel.

A: So, where next?

T: Well if we go south it means going through London.

A: Oh let's avoid London – the traffic is terrible.

T: I thought you wanted to go to Brighton?

A: Not specially. The south coast is going to be very crowded in August.

T: Well then why don't we go to Oxford, there's some lovely scenery around Oxford and then we're not far from Bath.

A: But what about the south west?

T: Another time! Let me add up the miles for this route, and see how much this is going to cost... and that's just on petrol before we even begin to eat or sleep.

Unit 6, Exercise 15 (p. 58)

1

WOMAN: You know the hairdryer isn't working?

MAN: No – I haven't used it.

W: Mm. And I want to wash my hair again tonight.

M: All right – I'll fill in this form. What's our room number?

W: Hm. Two four one.

M: Mhm. And the date?

W: It's the nineteenth.

M: And it's half past two, and – the – hairdryer's broken. Okay, I'll leave this at reception on the way out.

Listen again. [REPEAT]

2

GIRL: Right sir, I'll just fill in this card for you, and then the porter will show you to your room... That's Mr King – and you're staying from the twenty-third to the twenty-fifth – and it's a double room – number thirty-three – sixty-two pounds a night. And if there's anything else you need Mr King do please ask.

Listen again. [REPEAT]

3

HOTEL RECEPTIONIST: Jan, the man in room eighty-five asked for this evening's weather forecast. Read me what you've got will you, and I'll fill in one of these slips for him.

JAN: Right you are. That's October the sixth – cloudy and rain – and it's eight degrees C – forty-six degrees F. He's in for a nice evening!

HR: Thanks.

Listen again. [REPEAT]

4

BOY: I want to take my bike on the train.

CLERK: Hm. Where to?

B: From Liverpool to Leeds.

C: Right. Then the first train you're allowed on is the seven ten out of Liverpool.

B: Oh. What about the six forty?

C: No – no bikes on that one. And times back?

B: Yes please, around eight in the evening.

C: There's the nineteen forty-eight from Leeds.

B: Yes – that's fine – thanks very much.

C: Okay – you'll need to label it mind, and see the guard when... [FADE]

Listen again. [REPEAT]

5

GIRL: Excuse me please. Can you tell me how I can get a student coach card?

CLERK: Pardon?

G: How do I get a student coach card?

C: Oh right – sorry I didn't hear you the first time. You need a photo of yourself – well, two actually – two passport sized photos, and a note from your college saying you're a student.

G: And do I have to pay anything?

C: Yes, it'll cost you five pounds, but come back here and we'll do it over the counter for you... [FADE]

Listen again. [REPEAT]

Unit 7, Exercise 16 (p. 67)

ADMINISTRATOR: Somerset Study Programmes, can I help you?

MR YACOUB: Ah, good morning, I have seen your advertisement, and I would like to ask you some questions. You see I want to send my daughter to England.

A: How old is your daughter?

MR Y: She is sixteen years old.

A: Yes that's fine. Sixteen is our minimum age.

MR Y: I beg your pardon?

A: We accept students from sixteen upwards.

MR Y: Ah, good. Can you tell me what 'intensive programme' means please.

A: Yes certainly. We offer six hours' teaching a day – that's from nine thirty in the morning until twelve thirty. Then there's a two hour lunch break, and lessons again from two thirty in the afternoon until five thirty. Then on Friday and Saturday evenings there are various lectures.

MR Y: I'm sorry. Can you repeat that last bit please?

A: Yes. We invite speakers to the school on two evenings a week – Friday and Saturday – to talk about different things to do with British life and culture.

MR Y: I see. Yes I think I understand. And there are never more than eight students in a class?

A: That's right – sometimes not even eight, apart from the lecture evenings, when all the students are together.

MR Y: And what is the difference between full and part time?

A: Well – the intensive course I described to you is full time, but if your daughter doesn't want to study six hours a day, she can take either just the morning or the afternoon classes. That's obviously much cheaper.

MR Y: And can you tell me about accommodation please.

A: We can arrange for your daughter to stay with an English family. She would have all her meals with them. Or she can stay in a student hostel, and have her meals in the student restaurant.

MR Y: Mm. What is the difference in price?

A: The family accommodation is slightly cheaper, and as your daughter is only sixteen we would recommend her to stay with a family.

MR Y: Yes, I think that would be better. Can you please send me the details and the prices.

A: Of course. If you would like to give me your name and address then I'll put . . . [FADE]

Unit 7, Exercise 25 (p. 70)

1

TICKET INSPECTOR: Can I see your ticket please?

PASSENGER: I beg your pardon?

TI: Your ticket. Have you got a ticket?

P: Oh yes. Here you are.

Listen again. [REPEAT]

2

TEACHER: So, for your homework I want you to copy out the work we've been –

STUDENT: Excuse me please. What does 'copy' mean?

T: Copy? Um, I want you to write down in your exercise books everything we have done today. Copy it out from the workbook.

S: Right, I see, thank you.

Listen again. [REPEAT]

3

LANDLADY: Sven, can you pass me that tin opener please?

SVEN: Hm?

L: Over there – on the table.

S: This?

L: Yes.

S: What is it called?

L: Tin opener, a tin opener.

Listen again. [REPEAT]

4

BUS CONDUCTOR: Fares please.

PASSENGER: I want to go to, um –

BC: Yes?

P: Oh please. I have it on a piece of paper. How do you say this word?

BC: Eh? – Oh, Kew Gardens – you want Kew Gardens mate. Right, that'll be er, one pound twenty.

Listen again. [REPEAT]

5

RECEPTIONIST: How many nights are you staying?

GUEST: I don't understand. Can you say that again more slowly please.

R: Sorry. How many nights do you want to stay?

G: Oh, two nights please.

R: Right.

Listen again. [REPEAT]

Unit 8, Exercise 8 (p. 78)

1

MAN: Have you decided what we're doing this
evening?

WOMAN: I thought we might go to the cinema.

M: Oh no, let's go to the theatre. There's a choice
of three plays on at the National.

W: Okay, let's see what's on.

Listen again. [REPEAT]

2

GIRL: It's not very nice weather, is it – I don't really
want to walk around all day and get wet.

BOY: Well, let's go to a museum then.

G: Um – oh how about this one – all about
London and its history. It sounds a bit different
from the one we went to yesterday.

Listen again. [REPEAT]

3

BOY: We've hardly any money left you know. What
can we do that doesn't cost anything?

GIRL: Well we did the museums yesterday – I don't
really want to go to a museum again today.

B: Look, there's a free music thing on at the
Barbican. Jazz and rock 'n' roll. Let's go there.

Listen again. [REPEAT]

4

WOMAN: Have you ever been to this museum?

MAN: Which one?

W: This one – it's a cinema and television museum.

M: Mm. That sounds fun.

Listen again. [REPEAT]

5

MAN: Have you planned anything for this evening?

WOMAN: Well yes I have actually – as a surprise.

M: Don't tell me – you've got tickets for the opera!

W: Er, no – I booked a couple of seats for the
ballet.

M: Oh great!

Listen again. [REPEAT]

Unit 8, Exercise 20 (p. 83)

MAN: Are we going to see this new opera 'Tornrak'
next month?

WOMAN: I don't know – I can't decide – it's a lot of
money.

M: It's fifteen pounds each but there's a special
family offer if we take the children.

W: The children won't want to go, they hate
opera!

M: That's because they don't understand it – well I
vote we go – shall I fill in the booking form?

W: All right. When d'you want to go?

M: It's only on for one night – on July the

fourth – so there's no alternative date. That's
two tickets, and where d'you want to sit?

W: Stalls? Definitely not the circle.

M: Okay, so I'll put front stalls as our first choice
and back stalls as our second – they're both
fifteen pounds each so that's thirty pounds in
total.

◆ Further Practice, Unit 8 (p. 130)

ANNOUNCER: Welcome to the Eastway Arts Festival.
Visitors are recommended to use the Festival plan
which can be obtained free of charge from the
bookshop. All the events and exhibitions are
clearly marked on this plan.

The modern art gallery is situated on the
ground floor next to the main staircase. During
the course of the morning the Eastway artist in
residence – Nathalie Howell – will be available to
talk about her pictures. Visitors interested in
meeting Nathalie Howell should go to the far end
of the gallery.

Starting at eleven o'clock will be the first
concert in our international pianist series. This
morning the Russian pianist Vladimir Oblov will
be playing a range of work by Scriabin and
Chopin. If you would like to attend this concert,
please go to the recital room on the second floor
at ten thirty. The concert will start promptly at
eleven and no latecomers will be admitted.

For those of you interested in poetry, the young
writer Arnie Scott will be reading his own work
from ten o'clock onwards. Although best known
for his story writing, today Arnie has chosen some
of his favourite poems. Copies of his poems can
be bought at the bookshop which Arnie will be
pleased to autograph on request. The Arnie Scott
poetry reading will be in the piazza on the ground
floor.

The special children's entertainment will now
begin at ten thirty and not at eleven thirty as
previously advertised. The show is for children of
all ages and will include music, dance, and drama.
Due to the shortage of space in the hall, parents
are asked not to accompany their children, who
will be looked after by the Eastway staff.

Have you ever used a video camera? If not,
then today's your opportunity. Eastway Video
Studio have set up their equipment in the gardens
at the back of the building. During the day they'll
be filming various events, and visitors are invited
to join them. Try your hand at using a video
camera, and see the results of your work on one
of the TV monitors. For those of you
who. . .[FADE]

Unit 9, Exercise 2 (p. 87)

TEACHER: Right. Jack. Jack, let's begin with you – what's your hobby?

JACK: Fishing – every Saturday with my Dad. We go down the river, round about lunchtime and we stay there until the evening.

T: Even if it's raining?

J: Yep.

T: You must be very patient –

STUDENT: Lazy, you mean!

T: – just sitting and waiting.

J: Well, sort of.

T: D'you get bored?

J: No, there's lots of birds and things. There're other fishermen and we talk to them, and then there're people going past in boats.

T: What about you Sophie? Have you got any hobbies?

SOPHIE: Well, I collect various things, but um, my main hobby is collecting stamps.

T: How long've you been doing that?

S: Oh ages. I mean, I don't – um, I don't collect all kinds of stamps, because I'm particularly interested in certain stamps, so I don't bother with stamps which I think are boring – stamps with just people's heads, you know kings and queens and that, or buildings. I collect ones with flowers, any kind of flower – wild, garden – some of them are really beautiful –

T: Your stamp album must look very pretty then!

S: Mm.

T: Fine. Er, Leo – what about you?

LEO: Well, I don't have much time for hobbies, because um – I help in my father's shop at the weekend.

STUDENT: 'Cos he wants the money!

L: But – but I like playing cards, so I usually play cards with my friends in my free time. I mean we don't play for anything like money.

STUDENT: Ho-ho!

L: We usually play for matchsticks, and then at the end of the game we give them back.

T: D'you play any kind of board game?

L: Sorry?

T: You know, games which you play around a board, word games for example?

L: No. No.

T: Right. Now, has anyone got a really interesting hobby? Something a bit different?

ALL: Daniella, you have, go on Daniella.

T: All right, Daniella? Daniella what's your hobby?

DANIELLA: I keep snakes.

T: Goodness me! Isn't that rather dangerous?

D: No, not really – if you know how to handle them.

T: How on earth did you get a snake in the first place?

D: Well I wanted a pet monkey. And my parents wouldn't let me have one. So eventually my mother said I could keep rabbits, so we went along to the pet shop and the man showed me some of the snakes which were actually being fed with the rabbits.

ALL: Ugh!

D: And he let me hold a snake – it wasn't poisonous – and my mother, who by this time was saying 'Why don't you have some white mice, dear?' finally gave in, and agreed that I could have snakes. But the moment one escaped that would be it!

T: And has one ever. . . [FADE]

Unit 9, Exercise 11 (p. 92)

RADIO PRESENTER: [FADE UP]. . .and here is a roundup of today's sport. At the finals of the international tennis tournament in Australia, there was a third success in a row for the young Polish player Danuta Urbanik, when she won the women's title, beating Posy van den Bergh six three, six two.

In Beijing the men's table tennis tournament was won, as expected, by the Chinese. There was a surprise in the international hockey match however, in London, when the Canadians were beaten three one by the Finns. The Finns now go on to play the Russian team in Czechoslovakia next month.

At the first ever mountain bike competition held in the north of England the main race of the day was won by Thor Norvik.

And finally at the indoor swimming championships in Germany the gold cup for the best all round team effort was awarded to Bulgaria for the second year running.

Now here is Dominik Lawson with today's football results.

COMMENTATOR: In the first round of the Universe Cup, Belgium and Italy drew two all. There was also a draw in the match between Holland and Greece, with neither side scoring a goal. Both these matches will be replayed on Wednesday next week. In the other matches Egypt beat Scotland three one, and France lost to Wales by two goals to one. A late kick-off in the match between Brazil and Argentina means that we have no result at present but we hope to bring you this. . . [FADE]

◆ Further Practice, Unit 9 (p. 132)

MAN: That was a good game – you've beaten me four times on the trot now – are you free this weekend for another game? – then maybe I could beat you for a change!

WOMAN: I don't know –I'm getting a bit bored with all

this exercise. I think I'm going to take up something where I can sit down and read – like fishing.

M: You've got to be joking – you're one of the best tennis players in the club.

W: So what? There're loads of other things I could be doing – I hardly ever go to the cinema or the theatre.

M: But you don't like the cinema or the theatre.

W: That's not true – I just never have the time.

M: You could come during the week with the crowd from the office.

W: You know I can't – most evenings I have to work late.

M: Okay then, let's give next weekend a miss – let's do something completely different, let's go running or swimming.

W: Look, I've already said – I'm going to try fishing.

M: I didn't think you were serious. Fishing! You don't do anything – you just sit there.

W: Don't be silly – it's an art.

M: Oh yes?! And what d'you do with the fish when you've caught them – eat them I suppose.

W: No, you throw them back in – the skill lies in catching them in the first place.

M: Well don't expect me to come with you every weekend.

W: I don't! In fact I haven't asked you to come with me. I shall be going with John.

M: Oh I see – that's your game is it – I might've guessed.

Further Practice, Unit 4 (p. 122)

1 What will you find in the High Street?

GIRL: Excuse me, is there a take-away restaurant in this town?

MAN: Um – there's a fish and chip shop at the bottom of the High Street, but I don't think it opens until the evening.

G: Mm, thank you.

Listen again. [REPEAT]

2 What do they order?

WAITRESS: Are you ready to order, Sir?

MAN: Yes please. I'll have a hot chocolate.

GIRL: And I'll have a lemon tea and chocolate cake.

Listen again. [REPEAT]

3 What has the customer brought back?

SHOP ASSISTANT: Can I help you?

WOMAN: Yes. I did some shopping in here earlier today, um – fruit and vegetables and –

SA: Yes I remember.

W: Well I don't think the milk was fresh – when I tasted it it had gone sour, so perhaps you could change it.

Listen again. [REPEAT]

4 What is the complaint about?

WOMAN: Excuse me.

WAITRESS: Yes?

WOMAN: This cup is dirty, and so is the teaspoon.

WAITRESS: I'm sorry madam, I'll fetch you a clean cup.

Listen again. [REPEAT]

5 What does the man buy?

MAN: Have you got any fresh peas?

SHOP ASSISTANT: I'm afraid we're sold out, but we've plenty of frozen ones.

M: Okay I'll have a bag of those please.

Listen again. [REPEAT]

Further Practice, Unit 8 (p. 130)

ANNOUNCER: Welcome to the Eastway Arts Festival. Visitors are recommended to use the Festival plan which can be obtained free of charge from the bookshop. All the events and exhibitions are clearly marked on this plan.

The modern art gallery is situated on the ground floor next to the main staircase. During the course of the morning the Eastway artist in residence – Nathalie Howell – will be available to talk about her pictures. Visitors interested in meeting Nathalie Howell should go to the far end of the gallery.

Starting at eleven o'clock will be the first concert in our international pianist series. This morning the Russian pianist Vladimir Oblov will be playing a range of work by Scriabin and Chopin. If you would like to attend this concert, please go to the recital room on the second floor at ten thirty. The concert will start promptly at eleven and no latecomers will be admitted.

For those of you interested in poetry, the young writer Arnie Scott will be reading his own work from ten o'clock onwards. Although best known for his story writing, today Arnie has chosen some of his favourite poems. Copies of his poems can be bought at the bookshop which Arnie will be pleased to autograph on request. The Arnie Scott poetry reading will be in the piazza on the ground floor.

The special children's entertainment will now begin at ten thirty and not at eleven thirty as previously advertised. The show is for children of all ages and will include music, dance, and drama. Due to the shortage of space in the hall, parents are asked not to accompany their children, who will be looked after by the Eastway staff.

Have you ever used a video camera? If not, then today's your opportunity. Eastway Video Studio have set up their equipment in the gardens at the back of the building. During the day they'll be filming various events, and visitors are invited to join them. Try your hand at using a video camera, and see the results of your work on one of the TV monitors. For those of you who...

[FADE]

Further Practice, Unit 9 (p. 132)

MAN: That was a good game – you've beaten me four times on the trot now – are you free this weekend for another game? – then maybe I could beat you for a change!

WOMAN: I don't know – I'm getting a bit bored with all this exercise. I think I'm going to take up something where I can sit down and read – like fishing.

M: You've got to be joking – you're one of the best tennis players in the club.

W: So what? There're loads of other things I could be doing – I hardly ever go to the cinema or the theatre.

M: But you don't like the cinema or the theatre.

W: That's not true – I just never have the time.

M: You could come during the week with the crowd from the office.

W: You know I can't – most evenings I have to work late.

M: Okay then, let's give next weekend a miss – let's do something completely different, let's go running or swimming.

W: Look, I've already said – I'm going to try fishing.

M: I didn't think you were serious. Fishing! You don't do anything – You just sit there.

W: Don't be silly – it's an art.

M: Oh yes?! And what d'you do with the fish when you've caught them – eat them I suppose.

W: No, you throw them back in – the skill lies in catching them in the first place.

M: Well don't expect me to come with you every weekend.

W: I don't! In fact I haven't asked you to come with me. I shall be going with John.

M: Oh I see – that's your game is it – I might've guessed.

Unit 10, Practice Test (p. 110)

This is the Preliminary English Test Practice Test. There are four parts to the test. You will hear each recording twice. During the test there will be a pause before each part to allow you to look through the questions, and other pauses to let you think about your answers. You should write your answers on the question paper. You will have twelve minutes at the end to transfer your answers to the separate answer sheet.

Part One (p. 110)
There are seven questions in this part. For each question there are four pictures and a short recording. You will hear each recording twice. For each question, look at the pictures and listen to the recording. Choose the correct picture and put a tick in the box below it.

Before we start here is an example:

What time does the film start?

WOMAN: Are you going to watch the film on television later on tonight?

MAN: I don't know. What time's it on?

W: Five past eleven after the late night news.

[5″ PAUSE – REPEAT – 10″ PAUSE]

The woman says the film starts at five past eleven. So the first picture is correct and the tick has been put in the box under that picture.
 Now we are ready to start. Here is a short recording for the first four pictures. Don't forget to put a tick in one of the boxes!
 Listen carefully.

1 What did the man buy?
WOMAN: Hi – you've done a lot of shopping – what've you bought?

MAN: Well I've spent all my money, but I didn't find the jeans I wanted – but I got a pair of shoes, a couple of sweaters –

W: Oh let's see.

M: – and a shirt.

[5″ PAUSE – REPEAT – 10″ PAUSE]

2 Where will the man wait?
MAN: . . .So, where will you pick me up?

WOMAN: Mm – on the corner near the bus stop?

M: No – it's difficult to stop there. Can you pick me up further along the street, by that row of seats near the park.

W: Okay.

[5″ PAUSE – REPEAT – 10″ PAUSE]

3 How did they spend their holiday?
BOY: Goodness you're brown – did you spend your holiday lying on a beach?

GIRL: No – I'm not keen on sunbathing – no, we hired a boat and sailed around the islands for a week – brilliant!

[5″ PAUSE – REPEAT – 10″ PAUSE]

4 Which is the woman's luggage?
MAN: Is this your luggage madam?
WOMAN: Yes.
M: Would you open that large suitcase then please.
W: Oh no that's not mine – these two are mine – these two small ones and that large bag.
[5″ PAUSE – REPEAT – 10″ PAUSE]

5 Which picture shows where the man was sitting?
WOMAN: Did you enjoy the show?
MAN: The show was all right, but I was sitting next to some people who kept eating sweets and on my other side the chap next to me fell asleep, and snored!
[5″ PAUSE – REPEAT – 10″ PAUSE]

6 Which watch does the girl ask for?
GIRL: I'd like to look at that watch in the window please.
MAN: This one? With the white strap?
G: No the one next to it – it's got a blank face and a black leather strap.
M: Oh yes, I know the one you mean.
[5″ PAUSE – REPEAT – 10″ PAUSE]

7 Where is the bank?
MAN: Excuse me, I'm looking for the nearest bank. Can you help me?
GIRL: Um – the nearest bank is in the square. Not far. Carry on along this street, and when you get to the crossroads turn right, and straight ahead of you you'll see the town square, and the bank is on the left.
M: Thank you very much.
[5″ PAUSE – REPEAT – 10″ PAUSE]

That is the end of Part One.
You now have half a minute to check your answers. We will tell you when Part Two begins.
[30″ PAUSE]

Part Two (p. 113)
Now turn to Part Two, questions 8 to 13. Look at the questions for this part. You will hear part of a radio programme about travel and weather. Put a tick in the box for each question. At the end the recording is repeated.
[5″ PAUSE]
Now we're ready to start. Listen carefully.
RADIO PRESENTER: And now it's eight thirty, and time for our traffic and weather report from Julie Dunster.
NEWSREADER: Good morning, and I'm afraid it's more bad news for those of you travelling into London this weekend. After yesterday's plane crash on the motorway near Heathrow airport, there are still long delays while police and firemen continue to clear the area. So if you're travelling into London from the west, be prepared to queue for two to three hours before getting into central London.
    Passengers flying into and out of Heathrow today can also expect long delays as airport staff try to clear yesterday's flights. Before travelling to Heathrow, passengers are advised to contact their local travel agent, as many flights are delayed by more than twenty-four hours. Most hotels in and around the airport have been fully booked by airlines trying to arrange accommodation for their passengers who would otherwise have had to sit in the airport overnight. So please, don't travel to Heathrow unless you absolutely have to.
    On the railways the picture is a little better although poor weather and thick fog in the south east mean that most trains into London are arriving late this morning. British Rail also advise us that trains between London and Edinburgh are very crowded and unless you reserve your seat you may find yourself standing for the whole journey. Seat reservations can be made at your nearest British Rail Travel Office.
    If you are planning to get away by sea this weekend, please note that there will be no eleven o'clock sailing this morning from Dover to Calais. Due to rough seas the first crossing will be at three o'clock this afternoon and not at one thirty as previously advertised.
    For further information about ferry crossings you can phone British Ferries on O five seven double four one nine.
    And one final word for those of you hoping to travel by express coach. In view of the bad weather conditions, many coach companies are operating a limited service only, with far fewer vehicles running than usual. So please check before you leave home that the coach you are planning to catch has not been cancelled. All in all I'd say that this is a weekend to stay at home but. . . [FADE]
[5″ PAUSE]
Now listen again.
[REPEAT]
That is the end of Part Two.
You now have a minute to check your answers. We will tell you when Part Three begins.
[60″ PAUSE]

Part Three (p. 114)
Now turn to Part Three, questions 14 to 19. Look at the notes about a public meeting. Some information is missing. For each question, fill in the missing information in the numbered space. At the end the recording is repeated.
[5″ PAUSE]
Now we're ready to start. Listen carefully.
COMMITTEE CHAIRMAN: Good evening everyone, and thank you all for coming. As you know, the committee has decided to hold this meeting to see what we can do to save our local hospital from being closed down. I would like to begin by suggesting what we can all do to help and then give you an opportunity to ask any questions and discuss things further.
    Now, first things first – what we need most is money, and lots of it. Why? Because we need as much public support as we can get. We need

money to advertise. We need money to print posters. We need money to buy T-shirts and badges so that we have our message printed on these too. So, I want you to start thinking of ways to collect money and I have here some suggestions to get us all thinking. How about organising a disco? We have been offered the use of the school hall free of charge – a marvellous opportunity to raise money and a popular one at that! How about some of you musicians among us organising a concert? I'm sure you would all be willing to give up a few hours, and there's plenty of help around to sell tickets and print programmes.

The committee is also hoping to organise a food festival in three months' time, but we need plenty of publicity to make this event a success. We need people to contact the local newspapers, local radio, and TV. Perhaps we can invite a celebrity, someone really famous to open the food festival. Maybe you've got some suggestions over whom we can invite, someone who will pull in the crowds. We want to persuade people to open their purses and give us their money and that way we can begin to fight to save our hospital. . . [FADE]

[5″ PAUSE]
Now listen again.
[REPEAT]
That is the end of Part Three.

You now have a minute to check your answers. We will tell you when Part Four begins.
[60″ PAUSE]

Part Four (p. 115)
Now turn to Part Four, questions 20 to 25. Look at the six statements for this part. You will hear a conversation between a man and a woman about moving house. Decide if you think each statement is correct or incorrect. If you think it is correct, put a tick in the box under A for YES. I you think it is not correct, put a tick in the box under B for NO. At the end the recording is repeated.
[5″ PAUSE]
Now we are ready to start. Listen carefully.

WOMAN: I went to look at those new houses that are being built near the sports centre on my way home from work –

MAN: Oh yes.

W: – they're really nice and the workmen let me have a look inside the one that's nearly finished – there's lots of space and it's got three bedrooms and a separate shower room –

M: – Mhm.

W: – and there's a good sized garden at the back, big enough to grow vegetables, and they're not that expensive when you think what we paid for this flat. – John, you might at least put down your book. Aren't you interested?

M: Not especially.

W: But why? I thought you wanted to move – I thought you agreed that this flat is too small for us.

M: No. I don't want to move. You're the one who wants to move.

W: But you said the last time your brother stayed it was impossible without an extra bedroom.

M: You said it was impossible – not me. I like this flat. And it's very convenient. I can walk to work.

W: You could still walk to work if we moved.

M: It's much further, and it'd be far too noisy near the sports centre.

W: You haven't even seen the houses, and it's not exactly quiet living on this main road.

M: Well we chose this flat together you know, and you didn't mind the noise from the main road then. I seem to remember you liked the idea of being on a bus route.

W: I do. It's simply that we need more space. I hate not having a spare bedroom. John at least come and have a look at the houses. Please. Just for me?

M: Oh very well then. But I'm only going to look – no more – and don't expect me to change my mind because I like it where we are.

W: Okay okay. We'll just look!

[5″ PAUSE]
Now listen again.
[REPEAT]
That is the end of Part Four. You now have twelve minutes to check and transfer your answers to the separate answer sheet.

Acknowledgements

Special thanks due to Sue Garvin for her helpful comments and suggestions on the Teacher's Book.

Additional thanks to the many students who contributed to the Further Practice materials. Especially thanks are due to the following students who provided sample answers: Jose Filipe Barrancos, Liliana Bonini, Hélène Cahuzac, Christine Chaleil, Patricia de Oliveira Fernandez, Pablo Madrinan Grana, Syvain Laurent, Stefan Münch, Ami Nagano, Suzana Parreira, Beatriz Suarez Rodriguez, Emmanuelle Roussarie, Alejandro Sierra Sanchez, Bulent Seyhan, Katharina Widmer.

The publishers would like to thank the following for permission to reproduce copyright material. They have tried to contact all copyright holders, but in cases where they may have failed will be pleased to make the necessary arrangements at the first opportunity.

Ace Photo Agency 29, 32; Aviation Picture Library 28; Stuart Boreham 28; Camera Press 32; Early Times 34; Howard Fried-Booth colour prompt Section 3; Robert Harding Picture Library 29; The Hutchinson Library 29; The Image Bank 28, 29; Impact Photos 32; Liane Payne colour prompt Section 2; The Photographers Library 28; Pictor International Ltd 29, 32; J Sainsbury Plc 20; Welsh National Opera 36; Janine Wiedel 32.